THE HABIT OF LIVING

A WAY TO CALM YOUR SYMPTOMS AND TO FEEL HAPPY

by Ernest Mastria, Psy.D.

D1059716

First Edition

Ocean Publishing Company
213 9th Avenue
Belmar, NJ 07719

Website: www.drmastria.com
Copyright © 2000 by Ernest Mastria, Psy.D.

ISBN: 0-9714037-0-8

Library of Congress Control Number: 2001118929

Cover Design by Clea Carchia-Vaco
Photography by Annette C. Dailey

For information and additional copies:
Ocean Publishing Company
213 9th Avenue
Belmar, NJ 07719
USA

OceanPublishing@aol.com

Printed in the United States of America
September 2001

MArK

Best wishes

For a Happy

Birthday

Your friend

Dave S

10-27-01

Dedication

This book is dedicated to the memory of my friend Rose,
who taught me to be expressive
and to love clouds.

Acknowledgments

Special thanks to Annette Dailey, whose inexhaustible energy and dedication to this project made *The Habit of Living* possible, to my sister, Dr. Marie A. Mastria, who helped to convert my words into language, to Clea Carchia-Vaco, for her generosity and talent, to Dr. Erich Labouvie, whose frustration with the current theories and treatments of psychological symptoms resulted in a professional point of view concerning Attention Training, to Buddy and Patty who made suggestions to this project, to Kevin Swift, who made technology appear simple, and to all the people that I've seen over the years who suffered symptoms and were willing to try something different.

Points of View

"After previous treatments with a number of doctors, I feel with Dr. Mastria's technique I am experiencing a sense of control over my symptoms. The emphasis on increased attention is most enlightening, and the creation of a new habit and style of thinking make me much more aware of what is around me, thus creating a decrease in symptoms. I am one of his many successful treatments."
B.C., *Attention Trainee*

"Dr. Mastria's form of treatment which concerns an emphasis on increased attention in the present and the creation of a new habit or style of thinking is innovative and so simple – BUT IT WORKS."
O.L., *Attention Trainee*

"Dr. Mastria helped me to regain control of my life so that I can live the way I want to. Life is good."
S.C., *Attention Trainee*

"I believe Dr. Mastria's form of treatment is effective, all-encompassing and right on target. I recommend it highly."
J.Z., *Attention Trainee*

"What I find so fascinating is how simple the whole process is. I am so grateful to enjoy my life and relationships with loved ones again."
N., *Attention Trainee*

"I feel that Dr. Mastria has brilliantly explained the mechanism of all psychological discomfort."
N. C., *Attention Trainee*

Notice to the Reader

Although every story in this book is true, I have changed my people's names and identifying characteristics to protect their privacy. They, like me, felt a great desire to help others who may be suffering to know that there is hope.

The information contained in this book is not considered medical advice and is strictly the opinion of the author obtained through years of research and study. This book is offered to you as an alternative to the pain of Reflexive Attention Diversion. As with all such programs, you should consult your mental health doctor or other mental health professional before disbanding any other treatment or undertaking this program.

I wish you great success on your journey.

CONTENTS

THE HABIT OF LIVING

Enjoy your journey.

Foreword

A journey is a passage from one place to another. The place may be one of time, position, or concept. Sometimes, you may not realize where you've been until you arrive at your destination. Other times, you may not even know that you were on a journey. I arrived at my destination in early 2000. It was then that I realized where I was. I was inside a dream. I wanted to find the cause of psychological symptoms since I began to study psychology in the late 60's. However, I didn't realize I was working toward that end until I attained it.

Savoring the moment, I reviewed my years of study and practice. It was then that I understood I had traveled a journey into the land of the mind. It was a long one of over thirty years with many stops along the way, and was, by no means, a straight line. There were many twists and turns, many distractions. Some turns attracted my attention away from psychology and my dream, but somehow I always returned.

I had always known I was different, especially as compared to other doctors. They used the techniques of analysis, behavioral methods, and cognitive restructuring. I realized I was doing something other than what was traditional, but it was in my work with my patients that the difference between the more conventional doctors and me became most evident. I didn't realize how much until just recently.

However, now that I can see the years in an overview, what is most amazing to me is how the whole journey took place and how all the pieces fit together to bring me to where I am. It was then that I decided I needed to write down the experience and share my method with others.

This book is an account of my journey. It is a record of how I found an answer to the question that was always on my mind. Not in a focused way but in the back of my mind, like when you find a thing in a store that you haven't actively searched for but has you delighted when you happen upon it.

From the eerie experience of a mysterious redheaded woman who haunted my thoughts and signaled the beginning of my journey, to the pain of some of the people on whom I used the method and who pushed me to work harder to find the correct answer, the journey has been a unique one. This account chronicles my disappointments and my successes. Mostly, the book is intended to give you information. I want you to have a choice. My hope is that I have, in fact, found what I searched for: a single cause of psychological symptoms and a single method to eliminate the pain of those symptoms. If I'm right, then please use the knowledge in good health. Live happy.

Preface

The Bon Marché Incident-1968

Leaving New Jersey to attend college in Cheney, Washington was as exciting as a trip to a foreign country. I arrived in Spokane in the fall of 1967 and lived on the South Hill. My fifteen minute commute to Eastern Washington State College passed through a landscape of hills, trees and fields that seemed alien to a young man raised on the streets of Jersey City.

I chose to study psychology, a field that had held me spellbound since the days when I marveled at *The Three Faces of Eve, Psycho, Snake Pit* and an account of the life of Sigmund Freud and his strange dreams. The more I studied, the more I began to question the onslaught of personality theories offered to explain individual differences. I finally realized that psychology had no set of standard answers to address the symptoms that people suffered, and only offered a variety of theories and techniques as possible explanations and treatments. Which theory a psychologist applied depended on the likelihood of its success in that particular case. The "whatever works" attitude in psychology had me somewhat bewildered and disappointed, but at the same time excited about delving into the causes of the strange and often bizarre symptoms that I had read about. Since childhood, I loved to figure out how things work, not mechanical things but concepts and abstractions. Psychology offered me a journey into the unknown region of the mind and into the reasons why some people behave as they do.

There had to be something that caused Eve and Norman to behave as they did and to have Sigmund experience his disturbing dreams of his mother. The movies didn't clearly explain the sources of the symptoms that Eve and Norman encountered, and *Snake Pit* only pointed out the desperate need for a treatment that worked. I knew that the answer had to be simple and right under my nose, but what could it be?

My questions concerning psychology were nourished by the social awareness that had grown throughout the country. The revolution of thought and behavior flourished in 1968 and seemed to grow stronger as the year progressed. The spirited thoughts and emotions of change intensified as the ideas of peace and love became commonplace on the streets and in conversation wherever people gathered. The time was wide open for the deluge of opinions and attitudes that opposed tradition, and in many cases, set the stage for new outlooks and standards for society.

These changes in attitude were reflected in how young people dressed and lived. Tie-dyed tee shirts, bell-bottoms, and long hair were the uniform of the "Flower Power" movement while lava lamps, black lights and psychedelic posters decorated apartments. Everywhere, everyone asked questions. You could become acquainted with people on the street without fear of being mugged. It was a wonderful time to explore and discover in an atmosphere of cooperation and hope. On campus and off, feelings were strong and ideas bold. Young people searched for better ways to live together and to make the world a happier place. Civil rights and Vietnam demonstrations opposed the establishment and were sometimes met with violent retaliation in an effort for social order to maintain control over the rapidly changing attitudes and values that were common in the late 60's.

The fluctuations in attitudes and behaviors during 1968 were reflected in my thinking concerning psychology. On the one hand, I was fascinated by the different theories of personality. I was amazed at the marvelous structure that Sigmund Freud invented to explain how symptoms developed. His theory seemed to clarify everything from anxiety to hysteria. B.F. Skinner's explanation of behavior by operant conditioning made logical sense. When a behavior felt good to an animal or human, it was likely to be repeated. On the other hand, my thoughts concerning psychology were in turmoil. At times, I could actually feel the fight in my mind between the conceptually based Freudian theory and the nuts and bolts of Skinner's Behavioral Model. I was frustrated with the lack of consistency in the field and I wanted something to believe in. I wanted a method of treatment that worked every time.

I don't know if it was my confusion about psychology or my reaction to the extremes of 1968, but my thoughts seemed to parallel the up and down, peace and love and violence of the year. Nineteen sixty-eight witnessed a closeness among people that was cemented by a feeling of brotherly love. But 1968 also saw the assassinations of Dr. Martin Luther King Jr. and Bobby Kennedy, and "the whole world was watching" the horrific riots at the Democratic Convention in Chicago. It was a time when you had to choose sides between the establishment and "Flower Power." Nineteen sixty-eight was a scary time when confrontation between tradition and the social revolution clashed on every front in America, "from sea to shining sea." However, the young people's hope for peace and love eventually grew and blossomed as a result of the peaceful gathering at Woodstock in 1969. For many, Woodstock would become the banner that signaled "Flower Power" had survived the struggles of 1968.

Putting aside my thoughts of 1968, Sigmund Freud, B.F. Skinner, and social change, I looked forward to the upcoming weekend. It was a Saturday morning. My studies were up-to-date and I had no trip planned for the weekend. It was one of those days that I had totally to myself. Dressed in jeans, a tie-dyed shirt, teepee crawlers and a leather sash belt, I decided to go downtown and "people-watch." The day was brilliant. The sun was strong for autumn and people were casually walking, enjoying the weather and the dance of sunlight on the ripples of the Spokane River that runs through the center of town, transforming the bustling city into a picture postcard.

The sound of the river provided a natural background for the street musicians who played popular songs and originals that focused on the undeclared war, civil rights, the motives of the government and other social issues. Music was a wonderful vehicle for the exchange of ideas during the late 60's. From rock to protest to soul to folk to concept, music provided impetus and vitality to the social movement that propelled the 60's into history as a time and generation like no other. The peace and love era was fueled by the most daring musical revolution since Elvis Presley. Groups like the Beatles, Moody Blues, the Stones, Cream, and many others focused on society's attitudes and values. The messages sent to the young by musicians were taken seriously and often became the standards for new cultural directions and artistic endeavors.

The music, the brilliant day, the sound of the Spokane River and the atmosphere of change filled me with excitement. Somehow, I knew that there was no better time to be alive and twenty years old. The knowledge that the same attitude of free, open thinking was occurring in all parts of the United States at the same time was intoxicating. The intellectual fight for freedom from sameness and tradition brought me back to my question concerning psychology. What could be done for people with symptoms so severe that the system seemed pressured to plead "uncle" and to resort to medicating the suffering into a starry-eyed oblivion? While my thoughts of the burdened psychological dilemma remained in the back of my mind, they hadn't the power to stop the influx of light, movement, music, warmth, and sensation that flooded my body.

It was in this most wonderful state of mind that I decided to enjoy one of my favorite pastimes, going to the Bon Marché and checking out the new albums released since I had been at the store the week before. The Bon Marché is a large department store similar to Macy's in New Jersey. I frequently visited the store because it was familiar and felt like an old friend. Entering, I traveled in the direction of the record department. I had been there so many times that my movement was automatic. Passing the counters on the way to my destination, I encountered an older woman who walked with a cane. She was startled at my approach and I couldn't help wondering if my long hair, beard and how I dressed frightened her; or if her caution was automatic and served as a general protection to preserve her frail physical structure. I wondered if she might represent other Americans who viewed the change of the 60's as a threat to the familiar and traditional, with hippies as a symbol of that threat.

Leaving her behind, I reached the record display and found myself in heaven. The Jefferson Airplane, Dylan, the Stones, Hendrix and, of course, the Beatles, were all there. To my surprise, I found albums that I had searched for and had believed to be off the shelves and out of existence. This day was turning out to be "the best."

As I continued to sort through the generous supply of albums, I noticed a movement out of the corner of my eye and to the right. It was there, then gone. I paid little attention and went back to my labor of love. Then it was there again. This time I turned toward the movement. I saw a woman approximately fifteen feet from me. She was slender, maybe in her early thirties, and dressed in a gray business suit. Her red hair was shoulder length and curled in. She had electric blue eyes that were fixed on me, and her lips were turned up at the corners in a subtle but warm smile. Her attention was totally on me, and she seemed oblivious to the activity that surrounded us. There was no doubt in my mind that she was attracted to me. I don't know whether it was my surprise, her forwardness, or the idea that a beautiful, conservative-looking woman could be attracted to a hippie who looked like me, but I felt quite nervous.

I'm uncertain as to how long the next series of events took to occur. I believe it was only seconds, but it seemed like an eternity. I looked at the woman, who maintained the same seductive expression, and suddenly, my vision became foggy and tunneled. I could only see her face; all else was blurred. Even stranger, I felt as if I was looking up at her. My vision cleared a bit and I could see that the counters around me looked high, as if I were a child. I felt four or five years old with all the vulnerabilities and immaturity common to that age. My view of the woman also changed. Although she remained smiling, I felt that she somehow had the power to reject me for some inadequacy or fault that was beyond my knowledge. My mind was crammed full with all kinds of thoughts that I couldn't clearly identify. There were so many but none at the same time. I felt connected but apart, there but gone. Was this how people with symptoms felt? It was terrible. My nervousness intensified and I thought, "I've got to get out of here." I turned away from the woman, harboring intense feelings of shame and embarrassment as I moved from the record counter and in the opposite direction from her. I got to the street and felt my nervousness decrease and my perception return to normal. I was an adult again, with a million questions.

I went to the river to sort out the experience but was only left with more questions. Did the glazed look that I often noticed in the eyes of nervous people whom I knew have anything to do with what I had just experienced? I got myself together as well as I could and returned home, still a little shaky. I looked to my psychology books for information that could explain my experience and found nothing.

By the end of the day, I was back to normal, but the experience of the redheaded woman never left me and haunted my thoughts from that moment on. I knew that I would have to find the reason for the experience and that the answer would hold important implications for the treatment of psychological symptoms. Little did I know how important the experience of the redheaded woman actually was for me, and the impact that it would have for the many who suffer symptoms.

Introduction

What would you do if you broke your arm? Not so difficult. You would visit the emergency room of your local hospital, probably have the arm set, allow it to mend for six to eight weeks, and you may need physiotherapy.

But what if you hurt your head, not physically, but mentally? What if you had an anxiety attack? You might not know what it was and could believe you were having a heart attack. You would go to the hospital emergency room and after nothing was found wrong with your heart, the staff psychiatrist might check your head to see if you were crazy. And you thought you were frightened thinking you were having a heart attack. What if you're a male and the psychiatrist is a woman? Would you have to talk about sex? Think how embarrassed you'd be if you had a sexual problem and needed to discuss it with her. Suppose she found that you had a repression from childhood and the problem involved your mother? Maybe it would have been better if you did have a heart attack? Wait. Remember what you heard on the five o'clock news? Something about a gene causing anxiety? "Yes, that's got to be it. I'm sick. Only one way to treat the sick. A pill. That's it! I need a pill. Wow! That was close."

However, what if your anxiety doesn't land you in the hospital? Suppose you just get nervous sometimes? Your family doesn't see you as someone who needs professional help, just someone who is a bit high strung, and who isn't comfortable around people. They've stopped trying to convince you that your fears are foolish and accept you as somewhat peculiar. Or, suppose you always feel depressed? Friends and family tell you to get up and do something, but you just can't. You know that they don't understand and you feel isolated and alone. Worst of all, you don't know why you feel as you do. It seems to have always been there but, as you've grown older, it's gotten worse. And, should your family finally talk you into seeing someone for professional help, who would you see? It's not like you're familiar enough with a psychologist or psychiatrist that you could call for an appointment as you would with your family doctor. You don't even know what psychologists do.

You've seen TV programs with famous people talking about their depressions or anxieties. They spoke of how taking medication, talking about the past or using some other technique put their lives back together, but you can't afford to see the doctors that they went to. You think about asking some friends for advice, but you feel embarrassed. They'd probably think that you're weak or something.

Finally, you decide to research what kind of help is available. A visit to Barnes and Noble gives you all the information you want and too much more. Book after book on anxiety, depression, relationships, kids and on and on. To make matters worse, there are so many different treatments for the same symptom that you could spend years reading. Finally, you become convinced that no one really knows what to do about your problem. You leave the store and go home even more depressed over your situation and anxious about the future. Guess you'll just have to live with it.

The confusion you may experience concerning symptoms and their treatment is not limited to the average person. Psychologists and psychiatrists also appear to be plagued by the same dilemma. In its effort to find a cause for symptoms, medicine theorizes that a defective gene may result in a biochemical imbalance in the brain, causing the discomfort seen in patients. Evidence for the idea comes from the effect of medication on symptoms. If symptoms decrease with medication, the notion is that a fluctuation in brain chemistry caused the symptoms. However, the fact that the medication reduces symptoms does not necessarily mean that the fluctuation in brain chemistry caused the problem to begin with. For example, let's say a person suffers chronic headaches. If the pain decreases when the person takes aspirin, could it be that the body is deficient in aspirin? But what if the pain returns and persists? Should the person continue to take aspirin? Maybe the problem would be solved if the person just wore a hat on hot, sunny days when he goes for walks. The point is that just because one thing accompanies another doesn't necessarily mean the first caused the second. In the medical case, the fact that medication relieved the symptoms may not indicate that the chemical surplus or deficit in the brain is the cause of the symptom. The chemical imbalance may actually be a symptom itself. The question is what caused the chemical imbalance in the first place?

There have been a number of other theories to explain the causes of symptoms. One popular theory is Freudian psychology, which delves into a person's background and history to discover why symptoms are experienced. For example, an individual may walk into an analyst's office, ask the doctor where her anxiety comes from and the doctor may say, "You tell me." This question signals the beginning of a long, arduous search into the individual's past (especially childhood) for repressed memories, sexual incidents and fantasies that have somehow stopped the natural development to maturity and the enjoyment of life. Eventually, the individual and the doctor usually blame the patient's parents for her current problems and she leaves the session angry over the future and depressed since the past can't be changed.

In an attempt to relieve symptoms, other theories and treatments focus on specific areas of the mind and body. One recognized theory of treatment is the Behavioral Model. Behavioral techniques focus on removing troublesome symptoms that interfere with certain situations such as riding in elevators or cars. The idea is to eliminate specific problems rather than search for an elusive cause. The criticism of the Behavioral Model is that if the cause of the problem is not eliminated, symptoms may arise in other areas some time in the future and could be even more troublesome than the original problem.

Another form of treatment, the Cognitive Model, is one of the more current theories directed toward the elimination of symptoms. Its techniques focus on what an individual thinks concerning certain situations. The goal is to change negative thoughts so that symptoms are not triggered. The problem, however, is to determine which thought patterns to change and how many patterns must be altered before a patient feels better.

The treatments mentioned above could require a great deal of time and may not necessarily solve the patient's symptoms. After all, what do you go to an expert for? You want to rid yourself of a problem as quickly and economically as possible.

Why is it so difficult to receive adequate psychological or psychiatric treatment? Why is it that treatment for anxiety and depression isn't universal as it is for, let's say, a cavity or a cut that requires stitches? The answer is actually quite simple. In medicine and dentistry, a procedure is found for a specific ailment and, with replication, the procedure becomes universal with continued success. In psychology and psychiatry, a procedure for a particular ailment is difficult to find since the ailment tends to overlap onto other disorders. So anxiety may become anxiety with depression, anxiety with panic attacks, major affective disorder with anxiety and so on. This means that a treatment for a person with one symptom may not be effective for another person with the same symptom because of differences between the two persons.

Traditionally, different schools of thought have clustered similar symptoms together, classified them into disorders, and theorized different causes for each. As a result, different treatments are employed for the same ailments. This state of affairs leaves the patient in a quandary over which doctor to see for what procedure and for what ailment.

However, suppose one looked for a common cause for all symptoms instead of assuming that diverse symptoms involve diverse causes? If a common cause was found could it mean that different symptoms might be treated with the same technique? Such a discovery would revolutionize the treatment of symptoms. It would help to remove the stigma associated with those who suffer psychological discomfort and would allow the consumer accurate information concerning available services rather than the current "hit or miss" attempt at "normalcy."

The following chapters present just that: a single theory to explain the cause of psychological symptoms and a proposal for a standardized intervention. With motivated adherence to the procedures described, many individuals will gain relief from symptoms. Some will require the assistance of a trained technician for guidance through the procedure. Whether you agree or disagree with the basis of the theory and intervention, the proposal will provide an alternative so that you may make your own decision.

The theory that I refer to as Reflexive Attention Diversion (RAD), and the method of Attention Training, are my attempts to reduce the pain and suffering that so many individuals experience as a result of psychological symptoms. The theory and method represent nearly twenty years of thought and research that had its origin with the redheaded woman at the Bon Marché Department Store in 1968.

Chapter I

Misery Loves Company

"Think of your many years of procrastination; how the gods have repeatedly granted you further periods of grace, of which you have taken no advantage . "
Marcus Aurelius

The individuals presented below were actual patients of mine referred by friends, neighbors, family members, other patients and doctors. Their hellish experiences represent their histories just prior to making an appointment with me. While their stories appear quite different from one another, they are similar in that, in each case, the patient experienced extreme discomfort. Many had long histories of therapies and treatments and all were highly motivated to end his or her suffering. What's most fascinating about their stories is that most of us may see a piece of ourselves in the patients' strange behaviors and their nightmarish thoughts. Aside from their awful experiences, all the patients are common people with a burning desire to be happy, just like you and me.

Jim was referred to me by his internist after he experienced a panic attack that took him to the emergency room of a hospital. At the time of the incident, Jim was 26-years-old and feeling on top of the world. He had landed an excellent job as an investment banker, was happily married, and loved sports.

Jim loved basketball and had always been a Knicks fan. He was given some tickets by a friend and was excited to see the Knicks play Boston. At the end of the workday, Jim joined his friends at the Garden. After some laughs and a couple of beers, the game started.

Jim felt great. He hadn't a care on his mind except to wonder when center, Patrick Ewing, would be well enough to rejoin the team.

Some time just before the half, Jim felt weak and "unreal." His vision became foggy, his palms became clammy, and he felt tightness in his chest. The Garden began to spin and the noise of the crowd became unbearable. He didn't know what was happening to him. He searched for an answer for the way that he felt and found one.

Jim turned to his friends and told them that he was sure he was having a heart attack. His friends helped him from the Garden and into a cab that took them south on 7th Avenue to St. Vincent's Hospital. The staff in the emergency room put Jim on a gurney, rushed him to a room, ordered tests, and attached monitors to his chest.

Jim's friends called his family and, by the time the attending physician received the results of the tests, Jim's mother, father and sister had rushed to his bedside. The physician spoke in a slow, authoritative manner that commanded Jim's attention. He explained that his heart was fine and that he had not suffered a heart attack. It was the physician's opinion that Jim experienced a panic attack and suggested that he see a psychiatrist.

With his recommendation given in no uncertain terms, the physician took a long, bored look at Jim, turned, and walked away to attend to patients who really needed his help. Jim left the hospital with his friends. He felt embarrassed to have caused such a scene, but mostly, he was ashamed that he had behaved foolishly and that his friends would now see him as crazy. Jim made an appointment to see me on the following Monday.

Sandy was one of my most interesting patients. He had prior treatment with approximately two-dozen doctors and was referred to me by a psychiatrist friend of mine. Jim, the psychiatrist, had been medicating Sandy with little result. He told Sandy that my unorthodox methods might be his last chance to reduce the terrible symptoms he was experiencing. Sandy had tried nearly every traditional treatment.

Sandy worked as a draftsman and was raised in a close-knit Italian family. He stood 5 feet, 7 inches and dressed conservatively. Sandy's major symptom was horrible anxiety. His mind was overloaded with negative thoughts and he worried about everything.

Sandy was extremely concerned about what people thought of him. Maybe he would say the wrong thing and offend someone. What if he said something that was misinterpreted? One of his major concerns was that he might do something to physically hurt someone. As a result, Sandy always crossed the street to avoid the possibility of bumping into a pedestrian walking on the same side.

Still worse, Sandy blamed himself for behaviors that he couldn't possibly have committed. For instance, if Sandy saw a woman who was boarding a bus across the street and up the block, he had an anxiety attack believing that he had touched her inappropriately. He worried that women were aware of his sexual thoughts concerning them and constantly felt embarrassment and shame despite the fact that he was too anxious to have sexual thoughts.

Somehow, Sandy developed extreme obsessive-compulsive behaviors that seemed to reduce his anxiety but ate up most of his day. From early morning until he fell asleep at night, he felt forced to perform repetitive behaviors that made no sense to him other than his knowing something horrible would happen if he didn't obey their insistence.

In the mornings, Sandy had to open and close his eyes exactly thirty times, then open and close the drawer of his night table another thirty times. Things didn't improve once he was out of the bedroom and into the bathroom. It took Sandy over thirty minutes to shave because he had to fight off intense anxiety caused by looking into the mirror and imagining that his face was melting into a skull. His shower took over an hour. He had to wash three times while fighting off thoughts that today would be the day that he would hurt someone.

At thirty-seven years old, Sandy lived with his parents ever since his marriage failed. His wife just couldn't put up with his strange compulsions. It was during his marriage that Sandy stopped driving. It began when Sandy had to stop the car to check for damage that he imagined might have resulted from hitting a pedestrian or another vehicle. Soon his wife was forced to drive while Sandy rode with his eyes closed until the couple had reached their destination. Finally, Sandy refused to enter the car at all. He would leave the apartment early and take a bus to meet his wife who drove to a party or some other function. It was shortly after Sandy had stopped driving that his wife became frightened of what was happening to her husband and left him.

At work, Sandy was the brunt of cruel jokes. Co-workers would take bets on how many times Sandy would open and close a drawer, or they would coax a female worker to act seductively toward him or say that he touched her, then they would sit back and watch Sandy have an anxiety attack. He was overloaded with work and was given the tasks that others refused or found distasteful. He couldn't concentrate and his memory was poor. Sandy's life was totally dominated by his anxiety and unwanted behaviors. Often, Sandy thought about how nice it would be not to be here any longer. Sandy was losing control, and he knew it.

Jenny was referred by her sister, Ann, whom I had treated some years earlier. Ann did very well with me and wanted Jenny to try to relieve the misery that she was living.

Jenny is 6 feet tall and, at one time, seriously considered becoming a model. At 48 years old, she was childless and had been unhappily married for 16 years to an underachieving husband. For the two years prior to treatment, Jenny had felt terror at the thought of leaving her house. She couldn't put her finger on it, but she believed that something "bad" was going to happen if she left home. She and her husband had argued over missing social events and their marriage was in serious trouble.

Jenny had seen her family physician concerning her "crazy" thoughts. He prescribed sedatives, which she had been taking for eighteen months. Her problem was that the medication was no longer working. As a matter of fact, Jenny's fears had intensified and spread. She felt fearful handling money, answering the phone and, most recently, she avoided the laundry room because she was convinced she would drink liquid detergent and commit suicide. Jenny felt that she was slowly being painted into a corner with no way out, and no way to get help. She couldn't talk to her husband about it; he thought she was losing her mind. Jenny took to staying in her bedroom during the day, frightened to venture into the rooms of her own house.

Sam was the nicest teen you could ever meet. He was polite, friendly and sincere and suffered some of the worst obsessive-compulsive problems imaginable.

Sam was a 16-year-old junior in high school. His classmates picked on him endlessly, saying that he smiled too much. To make matters worse, Sam's self-consciousness forced him to be inattentive and awkward, tripping over students' feet in the aisles of the classroom or walking into doors. His attempts to prevent hitting the ground when he stumbled brought waves of laughter from his classmates.

Sam's family life was stressful. He had decided to live with his mother after his parents had divorced. He and his mother argued all the time. He believed she treated him like a baby and didn't allow him to make his own decisions. Sam is an only child, and his mother had always seen him as being on the nervous side.

Although the ridicule at school bothered Sam a great deal, it was his behaviors before bedtime that troubled him the most. These included ascending the stairs to his bedroom by climbing three steps and then descending two while he touched the wall to his right and the banister to his left. During this ritual, he needed to place his hand on the wall in the highest possible position while, at the same time, maintaining his hold on the banister. If he felt that he had failed to complete a portion of the ritual, he had to begin the process all over again.

Some evenings it took Sam over two-and-one-half hours to climb the stairs. Once the ordeal of the stairs was over, Sam slept on a cot in the hallway with his feet positioned across the threshold of his mother's bedroom. Sam couldn't explain it. He realized that the behaviors were "stupid," but he couldn't stop them. All he knew was that if he didn't do them, the anxiety would start and something terrible might happen.

A case that initially appears somewhat different from the others involved 38-year-old Bob. At the time I saw him, he was happily married for fourteen years and had two wonderful children, a boy, 10, and a girl, 7.

On an ordinary Friday morning on his way to the bagel shop that he owned, a car passed a red light and struck Bob's Chevy on the passenger side. Bob was taken to the hospital and released on the same day. Five stitches were necessary to close a nasty cut above his right eye. Bob went home, called the shop and explained that he wouldn't be in. He relaxed on the sofa to watch TV while Betty, Bob's wife, made him lunch.

Bob had difficulty sleeping that night. He was up until sunrise, and when he did sleep, he had nightmares of the accident. On Saturday morning, Bob called the shop and explained that he needed a few days to recover from the accident. Bob slept most of the day and believed the sleep was responsible for his insomnia that night.

Sunday morning was beautiful. Bob decided that he could use some activity outdoors. He dressed in shorts and sneakers and went outside to mow the lawn. As he began cutting his first strip, he was overcome with thoughts that something "bad" was going to happen. He tried to shake them off, but the thoughts persisted and intensified until he felt disoriented. Bob left the mower where it was and ran inside the house.

Bob did not return to work and only left the house to make doctor's visits, and only if Betty drove the Chevy. However, what troubled him more than his sleeplessness, confusion, and fear of leaving the house, was the thought that he no longer loved his wife and children. As a result, Bob avoided his family and friends and no one could understand the change in him.

Bill was referred by a friend and came to me because he didn't want to take the medication that his psychiatrist had prescribed. Bill's symptoms embarrassed him; he believed they were a sign of weakness.

At 225 pounds and standing six feet, two inches, 25-year-old Bill was an impressive sight. His bulging muscles and violent temper intimidated people. Most days, Bill spent up to four hours free weight lifting at the gym. He didn't lift weights for pleasure or health as much as to add to his already menacing appearance. Bill's use of steroids increased his weight to 240 pounds in no time at all. He was bigger than ever and scarier too.

During the day, Bill worked as a mechanic for a city bus line and on Saturday nights he worked as a bouncer for a local nightclub. Disputes were common as the night progressed and patrons drank too much. Bill was always the first to place himself in the middle of the trouble and the first to violently toss a customer from the club. Bill had broken the jaws of two customers on separate occasions and was awaiting trial for each incident.

Single, Bill lived with his parents and sister who experienced Bill's anger through his impatience and temper tantrums. He tended to take their opinions as criticism, and his blind rages forced his family into vigilant silence when Bill was at home.

Bill's friends were everything to him. They were big, muscular and had temperaments similar to Bill's. On spring and summer Saturday and Sunday mornings, Bill played softball with them. He really didn't like to play, he always felt awkward and nervous. Sometimes the feeling became unbearable. The games frequently ended with near brawls when Bill took a joke from a player as a "put-down." On Friday nights, Bill and his friends went out to meet women and to instigate fights. It was on one of these occasions that Bill seriously injured three men in a dispute over a woman. As a result, Bill awaited a third court appearance and a possible prison sentence.

In an effort to reduce the probability of jail time, Bill thought it wise to seek professional help. He attended an appointment with a psychiatrist in Manhattan and was told that he suffered from mood swings that were the result of a biochemical imbalance in his brain, which might, in turn, reflect an underlying genetic disorder. The doctor told Bill that he would probably need to take medication for the rest of his life. Bill left the doctor's office more depressed and angry than he was when he had entered.

Sarah came to me from a co-worker whom I had seen a year earlier. Although Sarah didn't believe her symptoms very unusual, her co-worker talked her into seeing me at least one time.

At 44 and single, Sarah worked ten to twelve hours a day and put in four to six hours on Saturdays and Sundays. Her schedule didn't leave much time for fun and socializing, but that was fine with Sarah. She wasn't comfortable around people. As a matter of fact, she experienced nervousness and stomach upset whenever she needed to be social. As a result, she hid in her work and became a dedicated employee.

Sarah's rigid work schedule was a soothing comfort for her fear of social situations, but deep inside, she knew she was missing the flavor of life. She felt trapped and controlled by her work and her fears.

There had been no special man in Sarah's life since her divorce some 15 years earlier, until she decided to accept an offer for a friendly after work drink from Tony, a co-worker. Sarah felt her usual nervousness when she left work with Tony and while he ordered drinks. After he returned and while she sipped, Sarah noticed that she was somehow able to respond to Tony's comments. Her nervousness decreased as she drank more alcohol. This made the drinks go down more easily and quickly, and Tony ordered more rounds.

With the evening completed, Sarah went home tipsy. Although her bedroom whirled and her head ached, she was happy that her nervousness hadn't interfered with her date. She enjoyed Tony's company and her night out more than she had enjoyed anything in years. If it took a couple of drinks for her not to be nervous, then so be it.

Sarah and Tony began to go out regularly. Every Saturday night they drank together at the corner bar until closing. While Sarah's nervousness was not completely gone, she felt that it was under control. Not even her worries over the future or her fear of people mattered after a drink or two or three. Somehow, she felt different.

Although she didn't like to be with people, Sarah hated to be home alone. That's when the scary thoughts about dying came. But Sarah knew what to do. She took to keeping a six-pack in the fridge, and, after a couple of beers, the thoughts diminished and her mood lightened. On more than one occasion, Sarah questioned her use of alcohol but decided that she deserved her drinks after a hard day at work. After all, what was there to enjoy in life?

Although Sarah tried to stop her drinking, all she could accomplish was to cut down. When she wasn't drinking, Sarah spent her free time at the mall, running up charge accounts, forcing her to work more hours to pay them off. It seemed to Sarah that drinking and shopping were her only ways to forget that she felt out of control and so unhappy.

Pat came to me from her family doctor who had heard of my technique from some of his patients. Although Pat didn't like the idea of seeing a psychologist, she was frightened of her symptoms enough to try some sessions.

It was the sunniest of Fridays and the first long weekend in nearly a year that Pat was able to wrestle from the company where she worked as a shipping clerk. The car was packed and Pat could hardly wait to see her parents and her sister's new baby girl.

This would be the first time she had visited her family without her husband in the twenty-five years that they had been married. Pat thought about this and did some simple math to figure that she had not been alone with her parents since she was 19, the age she married.

Thinking more, Pat felt that her husband and two children had absorbed her. She always thought of them first, and they seemed to expect her to cater to their every need. Pat even took their dinner "orders" over the phone at work and made separate meals for them. It wasn't that she minded so much; she loved to make them happy. But every now and then, Pat felt resentment toward them. True, she didn't feel the resentment for any length of time since the guilt that immediately followed seemed to wipe out any anger. But she did seem to identify herself by her ability to satisfy her family's needs.

Pat continued to think of all this as she left the Turnpike and headed south on the Parkway toward the Jersey shore. She looked ahead to the Driscol Bridge that crossed over the Raritan River. Suddenly, her stomach dropped. Pat didn't know what it was, but she felt terror at the thought of climbing the bridge, as though it was going to fall or something.

The terror mounted as she drove to the apex of the bridge. She felt she was going to drive through the guardrail and right off the side. She felt confused and disoriented, as though she was going out of her mind. Pat pulled over to the right lane and, with no shoulder on the bridge, nearly caused a serious accident and created a massive traffic jam. A New Jersey State Trooper stopped and called for a tow truck to remove her car from the bridge and back across again so Pat could drive home.

Since that day, Pat had not been able to cross any bridge nor had she been able to ascend higher than the second floor in any building. Pat left her third floor shipping clerk job on the following Tuesday.

Like Pat, Fran also worried about pleasing others. Fran was a "caretaker," she worried about how people she cared for felt. She wanted everyone around her to be happy and felt it was her fault if any of them felt bad. Although Fran suffered many symptoms, it was her anxiety that brought her to me.

Fran really didn't want to be at her nephew's birthday party. She preferred spending her Sunday with her new boyfriend, but her mother wanted her to come along. It wouldn't be nice if she missed it.

Fran's mother had made decisions for her ever since Fran could remember. At 22 years old, Fran resented it. She knew that her mother loved her and meant well, and Fran got nervous when she had to handle things on her own. But she really wanted to be with Ted.

However, Fran's attraction to Ted bothered her. She thought she might be getting too close. She'd been "dumped" by guys before when they seemed to be done with her, and she didn't want it to be the same with Ted.

At the party, Fran began to gorge herself with birthday cake and anything that was in front of her. "Oh boy," Fran thought, she was gorging again. Fran thought of Ted's reaction to her weight as she leaned over the toilet with her fingers down her throat. At 5 feet 3 inches and one hundred and three pounds, Fran believed that she weighed too much. She spent most of her free time exercising to make up for the times when she stuffed herself with food. She really didn't know why she gorged; only that it seemed to ease her "boring" existence. Everyone told her she was getting too thin, but Fran knew she was heavy and wanted to weigh less than ninety-five pounds.

She always thought that people wouldn't like her if they got to know her. Fran knew that from the self-critical thoughts that constantly occupied her mind. It was strange; part of her believed she was a worthwhile person and another part thought her unacceptable. Sometimes it was like two people arguing inside her head. It seemed that her weight was the only thing Fran could control. She knew she wasn't in control of her life. Fran decided she would stop at the drug store and pick up some laxatives after the party. That would help.

Billy suffered some serious symptoms. He was referred by his internist who was quite concerned with Billy's behavior.

Billy's thoughts shouted at him. They called him "stupid," "loser" and all kinds of horrible things. He was 20 and a junior in college. He had terrible trouble concentrating on his studies and spent too much time in front of the TV tuned to the weather channel as he drifted into oblivion. Billy feared the wrath of God. Somehow, he believed that he had sinned and was "bad."

Whenever there was a change in routine, especially concerning weather conditions, Billy believed calamity was going to occur. One time he became so upset with a pending storm that he left the house to seek shelter at the local hospital. There, he felt he'd be safe. His anxiety was so high that the emergency room physician decided to sedate him and asked for a psychological consult. Finally, his father picked him up and brought him home.

Billy stayed away from people and they from him. He tended to behave oddly around them, saying strange things and acting as if he was talking to someone who wasn't there. Actually, Billy spoke to his thoughts. Sometimes the thoughts were like voices from someone outside his body. Other times, Billy saw things. He saw blood all the time, but nighttime was the worst. It was at night when Billy saw demons. He lay in his bed and suffered fear almost every night. If he was able to sleep, he had horrible dreams, and in all of them, he heard his grandmother say, "If you don't do what I tell you, it's because you've got the devil in you."

A completely different case from Billy is Jerry, who didn't have anxiety attacks and didn't feel especially depressed. Jerry, at 35, was happily married with three great children. He graduated from college with a BA in Business Administration and landed a wonderful job with a major computer software company. Jerry and his wife entertained frequently and were well liked by all who knew them.

Jerry loved his family. He, his wife, and the kids spent a lot of time together. They played games, vacationed, and enjoyed discussions concerning current events and community topics and values.

Jerry appeared to have all that he wanted, and largely, he did. However, he just couldn't shake the feeling that he could have done more. Somehow, he felt constricted, tight. Some mornings he awoke with his arms and legs sore, maybe the back of his neck felt strained. Even around people whom he thoroughly enjoyed, Jerry was a bit tense, not all the time, but sometimes. He felt that he "held back," unable to be spontaneous. At times, with friends his own age, Jerry felt young, immature, having nothing to say. Every now and then, he felt the same tension at work. Although he was totally competent, Jerry believed that he was capable of more, maybe a vice president's position. But Jerry had never made the effort to move up in the company. Somehow, he just wasn't living to the fullest. He just never really let go. Jerry will never need professional help; he's fine. But he will never be as happy as he could be.

The cases mentioned above are actual ones. The people are real and their pain intense. Most suffered unbearable discomfort that was all the more terrifying since none of them knew where it came from.

An attempt to find a common cause to explain the discomfort that each experienced seems like an impossible task. If we look at the individuals, we see differences in their ages, sex, symptoms, the intensity of their discomfort, their behaviors, and so on. Looking at the situations involved is even more confusing. The places where the discomfort occurred were as different as were the people involved. Other differences included the time of day, days of the week, objects involved, and so forth. It is no wonder that psychology and psychiatry are in such confusion concerning the cause and treatment of symptoms.

Looking for similarities, we know that each suffered forms of anxiety, depression and anger as well as unusual and unacceptable behaviors. We can see that each of the individuals experienced negative thoughts of calamity prior to the onset of their symptoms. But what produced the thoughts?

Looking more closely, we may notice that just before the appearance of the negative thoughts and symptoms, each experienced a decreased awareness of their surroundings. Their ability to intelligently know where they were and what was going on around them decreased. Each became engrossed in his or her thoughts and symptoms to the exclusion of the events taking place in the environment.

Take Sandy. When he was engulfed in the idea that he may have touched a woman, Sandy became confused, disoriented, and illogical. Although he could not possibly have touched the woman, in his mind he believed he had. Similarly, Pat became disorientated when she attempted to cross a bridge. Fran experienced this decreased awareness when she had to handle things on her own, and Billy became disoriented and confused when concerned over weather changes. The same pattern was true in each of the other cases.

Another element that appears common is that all the individuals experienced some form of fear along with decreased awareness and negative thoughts. Sarah feared interacting with people, Bob feared that something "bad" might happen, Sam feared not performing his rituals; even Bill feared that criticism from people might be true. But did the fear come from the thoughts, the decreased awareness, or both? We know that each of the patients felt fear in relation to the content of their negative thoughts, but did the decrease in awareness contribute to the negative quality of their thoughts?

The fear the patients experienced seemed to occur after awareness decreased and negative thoughts began. Should this condition be common to individuals with psychological symptoms, a very important assumption can be made. If awareness of the here and now is not allowed to decrease and be converted to negative thoughts of calamity, then symptoms cannot be triggered in response. The existence of such a process would mean a breakthrough in the treatment of psychological discomfort. Let's take a closer look.

Chapter II

The Habit

"Remembering always what the World-Nature is,
and what my own nature is, and how the one
stands in respect to the other..."
Marcus Aurelius

To understand how symptoms are generated, it is important to learn how intelligence works. Our starting point is to define intelligence. Here's our problem. It seems that intelligence is defined in many ways. Many people think of intelligence as IQ. Some think of intelligence as "being smart." Webster's Dictionary, 1995, defines intelligence as, "The quantity, exercise, or product of active intellect; intellect; knowledge; ability to exercise the higher mental functions; readiness of comprehension."

My definition of intelligence is a bit different from Webster's and the others mentioned above. To me, intelligence is contact with your environment or surroundings through the five senses. Intelligence also includes the processing of the information gained so that events in the here and now are understood and may lead to purposeful behavior.

Let me explain. Humans are born with a natural tendency to direct attention outward, toward the world. This ability requires sensory contact with the environment or one's surroundings. Through this sensory contact, you gain knowledge and comprehension of the environment. You may then observe differences among situations and behave appropriately to the differences you perceive. Intelligence is your capacity to interact competently with the environment. This interaction cannot function at an optimal level unless attention is directed outward, with full sensory contact to follow.

This definition assumes that all organisms possess intelligence, the required ingredient for survival. Even the one-celled organism, the amoeba, must have contact with the environment in order to survive. However, in lower animals, the processing of information is largely instinctive and reflexive.

Instincts are triggered by genetic information and prompt the animal to behave in certain ways to ensure its survival and the survival of the species. For instance, a mother sea turtle deposits her eggs on the shore of a beach, covers them and leaves the eggs to warm in the sand and sun. With time, the eggs hatch and the newborn turtles scamper to the ocean before hungry gulls can eat them. How do the turtles know how to find the ocean? This information is transferred to the turtle through genetic data in the form of instincts. Instincts release the needed behaviors necessary for survival at the proper time. In this case, it's the turtles' mad dash to the ocean and to safety. An instinct triggers the necessary behavior with no need for prior learning or acquaintance with the situation in which the instinctual behavior is triggered. To me, the important elements defining an instinct are time and no prior learning. In this case, the time is birth and the unlearned behavior is movement toward the sea.

Reflexes are automatic behaviors that are triggered by a signal in the environment. For example, the baby turtles instinctively head toward the ocean to swim away from the gulls, whereas the motor movements of their walking and swimming are reflexive behaviors. Reflexes require a signal from the environment and, like instincts, are involuntary or automatic. The turtles' contact with the sand signaled walking or scampering and their contact with the seawater resulted in swimming.

Let's look a bit closer at reflexes. Reflexes are involuntary behaviors that allow us to devote our attention to the world around us without having to worry about more basic matters, such as breathing. Some reflexes run our bodies and are referred to as autonomic. A few of these include digestion, the eye blink, recoil from pain, the knee jerk, the heartbeat, circulation of blood and salivation. Others develop after birth and provide economy for often-used behaviors such as walking while we speak to a friend. We don't need to expend effort to attend to walking as we speak. Still other reflexes enhance our lives and contribute to the expression of our taste and the development of our <u>interests</u>. Playing an instrument, catching a baseball, painting, riding a bicycle, dancing and gymnastics are a few behaviors that may become reflexive or automatic and contribute to the development of our interests into <u>skills</u>. With the mind and body working in harmony, we can perceive the world, think, and behave to our benefit.

Instincts have been controversial in psychology since the 1920's when it was believed that humans possessed between fourteen and eighteen instincts. Currently, both reflexes and instincts are not considered in the treatment of symptoms. However, I find reflexes to be quite important. Reflexes respond to signals in the environment without cumbersome consideration and intention. It is their rapid response that helps to ensure efficiency in our behavior. An example may be ducking when a ball is thrown at you by surprise or the swimming behavior of an infant when placed in water.

As humans, we are largely purposeful and intentional in our contact with the world. We use problem-solving and decision-making to survive a sometimes harsh environment. We learn to plan and carry out behaviors to our benefit. For instance, we make and wear coats to keep us warm in winter, cool ourselves with air conditioning in the heat of summer, and cross streets on green to prevent being hit by a car. We may plan to shop before or after rush hour to avoid chaos and inconvenience.

INTELLIGENCE

We are born with intelligence and the ability to think. Our intelligence develops as a result of our interaction with those around us, our environment, and our experiences. How we grow and who we are depend on the interaction of our genetic information and our life experiences, mediated by intelligence. This means that as adults we are able to place ourselves in the lifestyle that best fits our likes. We obtain employment in a field that we enjoy, marry a person who attracts us and fulfills our needs, and live in an area that we like, raising our children with our own style of love, and develop our taste into interests. In other words, we live our lives to the fullest within the structure of the rules of behavior set forth by the group of people with whom we live, our society.

Let's take a look at the mechanics of intelligence and how it works to have us maintain contact with the environment and to behave for our benefit. Intelligence contains two parts that are vital for our survival. The first is the thinking part. The thinking part consists of all the higher functions such as memory, problem-solving abilities, creativity, planning, attention and focus, concentration, comprehension and humor, among others. The second part is the physical part or the five senses, which provides perception of our surroundings. We see, hear, touch, smell, and taste the world around us.

Intelligence maintains contact with the environment through attention. Attention occurs when focus is placed on the environment. The result of this focus is awareness of the present, the here and now. Take a moment and be aware of your surroundings. Maybe you're sitting in the living room, in your favorite chair. You note the time and see the pictures on the wall. You can hear your children playing in the recreation room, and your husband or wife speaking on the phone with a neighbor. You're aware of where you are and what's going on around you. You look down, see that you've read the page of your book, and turn to the next to continue your reading. Simple.

THE PROCESS OF INTELLIGENCE

Our perception of the environment (the interpretation of what we sense and how we react and behave) occurs quite rapidly. However, there is a chain of events or a sequence that may be traced in order to understand how intelligence works.

The thinking part of the intelligence directs attention toward the environment through the five senses. The senses bring back information as a result of what we see, hear, smell, touch, and taste. We can sharply focus our attention or concentrate. We can retrieve or remember information from the past and relate it to the present or <u>current</u>. With all the information obtained, the thinking part can orient us to time and place so that we know and understand where we are and what's going on around us.

The very important results of contact with our surroundings and the major <u>characteristics of intelligence</u> are the abilities to see differences among situations and the capacity to accurately behave in response to the differences that we see. For example, a patient makes an appointment for Tuesday at noon. As a result, he shows up on Tuesday at the appropriate time for his session rather than on Monday or Wednesday. Or, he runs up to hug a family member rather than a total stranger. He arrives at his bank rather than the one next door to make a deposit, etc.

Contact with the environment allows us to express. <u>Expression</u> is interaction with the environment and occurs in three modes. The first is movement. Walking through the environment, stretching, moving a pen, catching a ball, and so on are all examples of movement or <u>motor expression</u>. The second is <u>verbal</u> or speech. Expressing an opinion to a friend or placing an order at a fast food restaurant involves verbal expression. The third and most used expression is thinking. Thoughts are continuous. Some <u>thoughts</u> have words and/or pictures attached to them, but most are simply attitudes learned over time in response to familiar situations so that they occur automatically without wasting attention, time, and energy. Expression is continuous, even during sleep. We are continuously having thoughts, mostly in the form of attitudes, in relation to our surroundings. However, since most thoughts occur so rapidly, we are largely unaware of their presence.

Expression conveys likes and dislikes through decisions, opinions, behaviors, and points of view. <u>Self</u> is composed of <u>taste</u> or likes and dislikes. To me, self is personality. Self is what makes one person different from another. The way in which people come to know one another is through self-expression. <u>Self-expression</u> is the process of interacting with the environment in a smooth, economical manner, according to your taste. The expression of taste creates a style from which others come to recognize the manner which influences your movement, thoughts, interests, and opinions. In other words, style reflects your taste.

WHEN INTELLIGENCE MALFUNCTIONS

The patients mentioned in the previous chapter experienced reduced awareness as a result of decreased attention or focus directed toward the environment. At these times, each experienced less intelligence or interaction with the world. Their ability to be purposeful and intentional literally decreased. They became less accurate in their perception and comprehension of their surroundings and more reflexive or automatic in their behavior. They were less able to express themselves and actually were prevented from expression by the negative thoughts and behaviors that they experienced. For example, when Jim felt "unreal" at the Garden, when Sandy thought he had touched a woman inappropriately, when Jenny believed she would hurt herself, when Sam felt compelled to perform his rituals, and when Bob believed something "bad" was going to happen - each had lost some contact with the real world. Literally, less information was coming to them through the five senses. They all felt somewhat disoriented to time and place and were responding to events other than those that were occurring in reality. The response of each patient was to his or her own negative thoughts with no basis in reality. For instance, Bill had no logical reason to anticipate that people would find fault with him, no one had actually criticized him. Sarah had no justification to fear people; no one hurt her, so that her use of alcohol to "soothe" her fear was unwarranted. Pat would never drive off the Raritan Bridge. Fran could control her life. Billy saw demons that weren't there in reality. Even Jerry's belief that he would "make waves" and offend people was unfounded. Jerry is one of the nicest guys who ever walked the face of the earth. All these individuals lost the ability to see differences in situations and therefore could not make intelligent judgments. All were responding to negative thoughts that had little to no basis in reality and the world. At the times when the negative thoughts occurred, the content of the thoughts was their reality. To varying degrees, all were living their thoughts.

REFLEXIVE ATTENTION DIVERSION (RAD)

What each patient experienced is what I call <u>Reflexive Attention Diversion</u> (RAD) from the environment. RAD is the same for all people with psychological symptoms. It works in the same manner and always results in symptoms. RAD is a habit or reflex, like a knee jerk or an eye blink. Its only purpose is to prevent expression toward events by reducing awareness of your surroundings. Reduced awareness eliminates spontaneous expression since events are not fully witnessed, and therefore cannot be completely experienced and responded to.

RAD is built on the misinformation that, contained within your likes and dislikes, is some flaw or badness that, when expressed, will offend and warrant some negative consequence, generally anger from another individual. Simply put, the bad habit is a tendency to take differences of opinion personally as angry acts or as criticism.

RAD automatically prevents spontaneity and, as such, is a "<u>bad habit</u>" in that it opposes the natural tendency for you to maintain intelligence or full contact with the environment. The bad habit distracts you from your surroundings so that expression cannot fully occur. Instead of full awareness of the environment, you attend to negative thoughts in the form of words, pictures and attitudes, and to other symptoms. As a reflex, the bad habit is out of conscious control and quite rapid in its effect. However, there is a sequence to the habit that may be traced.

THE CLASH BETWEEN INTELLIGENCE AND THE HABIT (RAD)

Figure 1

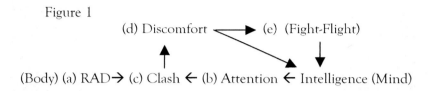

Expression is a continuous process since thinking is always occurring on some level. This would mean that RAD (a), or the bad habit, is constantly clashing with the natural tendency for you to maintain intelligence through attention (b) or contact with the environment or the world. The clash (c) between the two forces results in a friction, usually experienced as a mild tension or discomfort (d). This discomfort results in the <u>fight-flight response</u> (e), triggered when awareness is decreased by the habit. Since expression is continuous, the fight-flight reaction will be continuous.

The fight-flight response is a biological defense mechanism designed to protect you from harm. It is triggered when you perceive or sense danger, a condition that generates fear. Its effect is to mobilize you to either fight off the threat or to run for safety. For example, a cat sees a dog. The cat focuses on the threat, feels fear and either fights the dog if cornered or runs for safety. The cat's body enters a state of alarm, physically ready to fight for survival. With safety, the cat's body reduces the state of alarm and physical functions return to normal. In much the same way, RAD, through faulty learning and constricted expression of taste, causes you to perceive threat in the environment.

The interference from the habit is continuous and results in a chronic state of alarm that never really shuts down. This chronic state causes you to experience discomfort resulting in a constant state of urgency, an incessant over-vigilance toward threat that doesn't exist in reality. It is, instead, a by-product of the decreased awareness generated by the bad habit.

PROBLEM-SOLVING THE DISCOMFORT

Figure 2

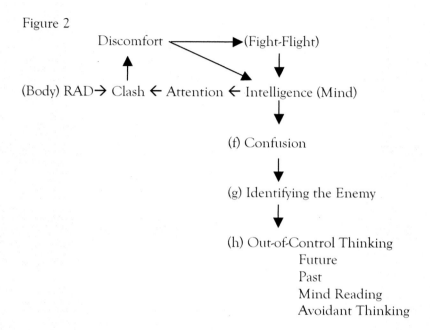

Intelligence is our most basic and primary survival mechanism because it functions to maintain contact with the environment. As such, intelligence allows us to problem-solve. The discomfort caused by decreased awareness becomes the focus of problem-solving by the intelligence so that you may return to a comfortable state. With RAD occurring, intelligence searches the environment but is unable to identify the source of threat in the here and now. Without an identifiable threat in reality, confusion (f) is generated. Confusion is uncertainty resulting from a lack of information and can spiral into extreme fear and terror. At all costs, the intelligence must solve the problem as to where the threat and resulting discomfort are coming from. In its effort to reduce confusion and to identify the enemy (g), the intelligence automatically redirects attention away from the environment and moves forward or back in time or behind the eyes of people to read their minds. These "out-of-control" (h) or "out-of-present" thoughts are nothing more than fabrications used by the intelligence to justify the discomfort of decreased awareness and to reduce the pain of confusion. "I know, when I go out something bad will happen." and, "In the past, something bad happened." and, "What will people think of me? They'll know I'm crazy or bad or different or something." Avoidant thinking occurs in low activity situations and results in a dazing off from reality.

At such times, with reduced contact with the environment, intelligence literally decreases. The intelligence no longer has optimal sensory contact with your surroundings and, as a result, cannot provide its primary function of smooth interaction with the world in the here and now. Literally less information is coming from the five senses. Vision becomes foggy or cloudy, hearing becomes hollow, sensation is numb, and smell and taste are virtually nonexistent. You can't concentrate or remember, problem-solving is impossible, and the two most important characteristics of the intelligence: the ability to perceive differences and to respond to the differences perceived, recede. You aren't able to accurately tell the difference between a thought and reality.

The content of the out-of-control thoughts must have some value or importance to you in order to justify the discomfort. However, without the accuracy and structure of intelligent contact with the environment and reality, out-of-control thoughts tend to spiral upward into the most disastrous scenarios. You're often left with a formless negative attitude of pending doom. "I don't know what it is, but I know it will be bad, and I won't be able to handle it."

The out-of-control thoughts have reduced confusion since you believe you now know the source of the discomfort. However, because the thoughts were used to justify a negative quality, discomfort, the thoughts themselves will be negative. Although confusion is reduced, you're left with a head full of negative thoughts.

EMOTIONAL REACTION TO THE HABIT

Figure 3

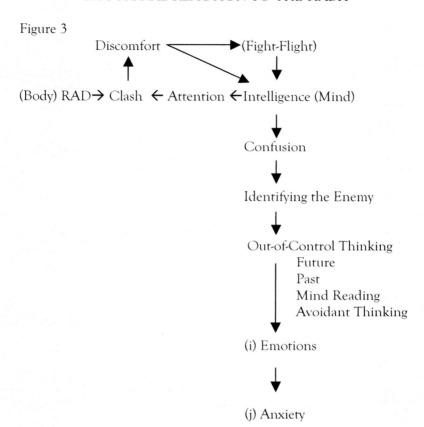

Discomfort ⟵⟶ (Fight-Flight)

(Body) RAD→ Clash ← Attention ← Intelligence (Mind)

Confusion

Identifying the Enemy

Out-of-Control Thinking
Future
Past
Mind Reading
Avoidant Thinking

(i) Emotions

(j) Anxiety

Negative thoughts trigger negative emotions. <u>Emotions</u> (i) are biochemical reactions to thought. They are literally slaves of thought. You cannot have an emotion without a thought first occurring. Most thoughts are <u>attitudes</u>. They are well-learned responses to familiar situations, and therefore, quite rapid in their response to events. They are so rapid that you might not even be aware of their occurrence. The emotion triggered by the negative thoughts is anxiety (j), and it is more intense than the original discomfort since the anxiety is now attached to a specific fabricated situation(s) or event(s).

Anxiety, generated by the negative thoughts, results from the fight-flight response in reaction to the perception that danger exists. Now, the body is in a heightened state of alarm, mobilized to deal with danger.

For instance, if I had an anxiety attack while riding as a passenger in a car that my sister was operating, I might view the car or my sister's driving as responsible for my anxiety. As a result, I would avoid riding in a car that she was driving. If I had to ride with her for some reason, I would experience increased anxiety during the trip since I would anticipate that something negative was going to happen, maybe an accident.

However, anxiety can also attach to a seemingly vague attitude. An example is an attitude of pending doom. Pending doom is not specific to a particular situation but to a feeling of a general terrible calamity. Actually, the anxiety associated with pending doom attaches to a future event; a time when something bad will happen. In the examples above, specifically, my sister will have an accident with me in the car in the future, and generally, something bad will happen in the future.

Anxiety can reach all kinds of intensities and be manifested in many different ways, from a dreamlike, unreal, pending doom, to terror that something specific will happen that can't be handled and will be followed by disaster. Regardless of the form it takes, anxiety is quite uncomfortable. Just ask anyone who has experienced it.

AVOIDANT BEHAVIORS AND DEPRESSION

Figure 4

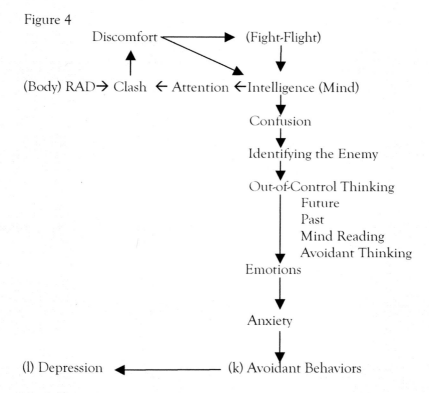

Over time, you learn behaviors designed to reduce the discomfort of anxiety. I call these avoidant behaviors (k). <u>Avoidant behaviors</u> have one function, to stop you from spontaneous expression. They force you to do what you don't want in order to reduce anxiety. Examples of some avoidant behaviors are saying "yes" instead of "no," not saying anything at all, avoiding situations totally, drifting or zoning out while in front of the TV, <u>compulsions</u>, lying and stealing, hostility, out-of-control thinking, <u>obsessions</u>, working too much, or any other behavior that has you avoid doing as you like. And they work. You're no longer in a situation to convey likes and dislikes so that the "bad thing"

contained within cannot offend. No "crime," no "punishment," and anxiety is reduced. The reduction of anxiety reinforces the avoidant behaviors and makes them quite powerful and resistant to change or elimination.

However, you realize that you're not living life fully and become self-critical, thinking, "I've always been this way, and I will never change." These thoughts stimulate depression (l) since you are not behaving according to your taste and therefore cannot experience pleasure. <u>Depression</u> occurs when you chronically behave as you don't like rather than as you like.

THE HABIT AS A MACHINE

Figure 5

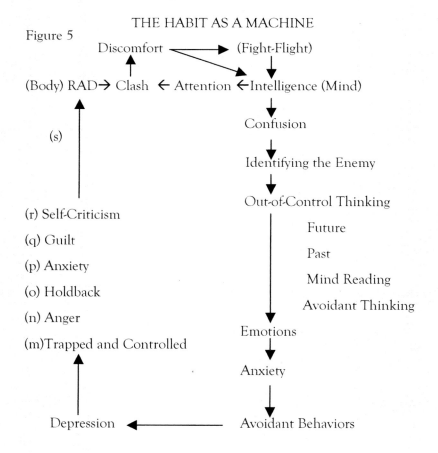

Depression has you feeling <u>trapped and controlled</u> (m) by this "no win" dilemma. Over time, you become frustrated with your monotonous, boring existence, and anger (n) is generated for living life without a chance of pleasure. However, since you believe expression to be an angry act, the feeling of real anger triggers intense <u>holdback</u> (o) and you avoid angry expression for fear of retaliation from others. But the anger intensifies, generating anxiety (p) over negative consequences, since the thought that the "bad thing" (expressing anger and offending) is close to occurring.

But the anger doesn't go away. It tends to build up. Seemingly trivial situations, like saying "yes" when you want to say "no" or saying "It's OK." too frequently, cause anger to accumulate. Sooner or later, you explode with anger over the dumbest situation and out of proportion to the event. Now, you feel guilty (q) and <u>self-critical</u> (r), all proving that you should not express. This string of events supports (s) the attitude that the expression of taste will lead to disaster, allowing the cycle of the bad habit to continue and to strengthen.

The complete sequence of the habit works like a machine, in the same way for all people with psychological symptoms. The only difference among those with the habit is which symptoms are dominant and the intensity of those symptoms.

Let's take some of Sandy's behaviors from Chapter One and see how the habit worked with him. Sandy experienced a chronic decrease of awareness as a result of reduced attention. He was always over-vigilant, constantly waiting for the "bad thing" to happen. Sandy lived with tension and nervousness, cautious not to do the wrong or "bad thing."

The habit attached to any of Sandy's thoughts, actions, or experiences or to the behaviors and attitudes of another person, which could possibly be evidence to Sandy that the "bad thing" was occurring. It would attach to the thought that he might have hit another vehicle or a pedestrian with his car, touched a woman boarding a bus across the street, made inappropriate advances toward a co-worker, not opened and closed his drawer enough times, or to any situation that could be an indication that he had expressed himself and the "badness" had emerged.

Although the out-of-control thoughts reduced Sandy's chronic confusion over what was causing his discomfort, they were negative, and Sandy experienced severe anxiety in reaction. As a result, Sandy avoided social events or situations that were unpredictable, where he might feel out-of-control.

During his free time, Sandy felt anxious since he could do whatever he wanted and expose the badness that lived somewhere inside him. In other words, he could express his taste and be "himself." He could watch TV, listen to music, call a friend and go out, speak with his family, anything. This condition generated a great deal of anxiety in Sandy.

In his effort to reduce anxiety, Sandy developed some strange rituals and behaviors to occupy his time and disallow spontaneous expression. One was his opening and closing dresser drawers or the refrigerator door. If he were to sit on a chair or the couch, Sandy would lower himself, then rise a number of times before he could settle down. The behaviors, no matter how strange they appeared, all had the same purpose: to prevent spontaneous expression and the "bad thing" from happening. All the time Sandy was engaged in his rituals, he was distracted from the environment and couldn't fully express his taste to any situation occurring in the present, since he wasn't totally experiencing events.

Sandy's avoidance did reduce his anxiety, but it generated depression since he was not behaving according to his taste. Sandy was doing what he didn't want rather than what he wanted. He wasn't enjoying his life; he was trying to avoid pain. His rituals, behaviors, and thoughts left him feeling trapped and controlled by his personal hell, without a hope of happiness. He felt angry and, at times, Sandy would blow up at a family member over the most trivial matter. He would feel guilty over the incident, become self-critical and would try even harder to hold back his expression, since he knew the "bad thing" inside would hurt the people whom he loved if it escaped from his lips or from his body.

Most interesting concerning Sandy's dilemma was the habit's effect on his intelligence. Sandy is actually a very intelligent man. However, with his attention chronically diverted from the environment, his intelligence literally decreased. With less attention and focus directed toward his surroundings, Sandy's senses decreased in clarity. He couldn't concentrate or remember well. His behavior was tight and awkward. He was less able to make decisions, plan, or problem-solve. He felt insecure, inadequate, and out-of-control of his life and his feelings. At times when the habit intensified, Sandy's intelligence decreased even further and he became <u>disoriented</u>, not really sure where he was and what was going on around him. He had one thought only, to "get out of this place" at any cost.

Most remarkable concerning Sandy's decrease in intelligence was his inability to see differences and to <u>respond</u> to the differences that he saw. When Sandy thought he touched a woman who was boarding a bus across and up the street, the thought became his reality. The fact that he couldn't possibly have touched the woman held no weight. To Sandy, he had touched the woman and he would be punished for the act.

Sandy's basic problem was the faulty belief system that contained within his taste was some "badness" which, if expressed, would hurt those around him, and he could expect angry retaliation from them. Since he didn't know what the "<u>bad thing</u>" was, he looked for it everywhere, regardless of logic and physical reality.

But what about some of the others? Their behaviors and situations seemed different from Sandy's. But not really. Jenny's habit attached to the thought that something she couldn't control would happen if she left her house to do as she wanted. The thought, that something "bad" in her taste would force her to kill herself, had Jenny feel out-of-control of her mind and her body. The last thing in the world Jenny would do would be to hurt herself or anyone else for that matter. But again, reality has nothing to do with it. With decreased intelligence, Jenny couldn't see differences among situations, and her thoughts became real. Her avoidance finally had her holed up in her bedroom to reduce the possibility that the "bad thing" might happen. Although avoidance initially reduced her anxiety, it led to depression, frustration and further anxiety since she realized she couldn't be safe from her own thoughts.

Jenny's symptoms followed the sequence of the habit. She experienced chronic holdback that increased in intensity whenever she was in a situation to express. Since expression constantly occurs as a result of mere existence, Jenny was always feeling tense and anxious. Since a source for her discomfort could not be identified in the current, confusion was generated. Jenny's intelligence automatically attempted to justify her discomfort with out-of-control thoughts. As a result, Jenny's thoughts identified the enemy with content that possessed certain characteristics. They had to be of high value or they wouldn't be capable of attracting Jenny's attention. They needed to be negative since they were used to justify discomfort and they had to be personal in order to pertain to Jenny's taste. Since the habit indicated that badness was contained in Jenny's taste and would be exposed should she express, her out-of-control thoughts would have to do with behaviors that were contrary to Jenny's morals and value system. In Jenny's case, it was suicidal behavior and fear of being hurt. These thoughts effectively prevented Jenny from expressing her taste and enjoying life.

Sarah's avoidant behaviors included overworking and alcohol abuse. Although her anxiety decreased as a result of her avoidance of expression - depression and frustration followed. The same was true for Pat and Fran. As a matter of fact, the sequence was the same for all the individuals discussed. With Billy, the habit was so intense that he actually lived his thoughts, hearing and seeing them as voices and demons and other horrific hallucinations. In an effort to decrease confusion, his out-of-control thinking conjured up demons to represent the "bad thing" inside Billy's taste. His thoughts were so intense they flooded his senses to the point where he actually saw and heard them.

Three of the individuals mentioned may appear different from the others. Bob didn't have the habit prior to his traffic accident. It was the accident that triggered RAD and his symptoms. This special case will be discussed in the next chapter.

Bill's dominant symptom was anger. This also appears different from the others who seemed hesitant to express their thoughts and feelings. However, Bill's habit is the same as all the others. Bill felt anxious over self-expression, and even though he did tend to hold back for fear of offending, his major symptom was to take differences from others as criticism. As a result, Bill walked around with a chip on his shoulder, constantly anticipating that people would find fault with him. Bill, like the others, responded to his thoughts rather than to reality. Since his thoughts were negative, his emotional reaction was negative. Bill experienced angry hostility and aggression when it wasn't necessary.

Jerry was never a patient of mine. Actually, Jerry is a friend. He's basically a happy guy with a wonderful life and future. Jerry will never need to have medication, his background analyzed or require behavioral treatment. His symptoms were not as intense as my patients', but his habit was the same, with the same sequence. He just wasn't living life to the fullest. Jerry held back expression just a bit. He didn't laugh as loudly as he felt, he didn't walk as loosely as he could, he sat up a little too rigidly, he passed up throwing a ball at the stacked bottles at a carnival, he wouldn't apply for a better position that he was qualified for. He just wasn't fully there, living moment by moment. Jerry was like so many of us, oversocialized. Jerry worried about breaking rules that simply didn't exist.

All those discussed above had the same habit, which worked in the same way and produced the same symptoms. The intensity of the habit and its influence was different among the individuals. The content of the thoughts was different. The situations the habit attached to were different and the dominant symptoms were different. However, beneath the differences, each experienced a chronic decreased awareness toward the environment and the same sequence of symptoms with a reduction of intelligence. For all, the habit was based on the misinformation that <u>differences of opinion</u> are not points of view, but rather, angry acts which will offend, with negative consequences to follow.

So where does the habit come from? How is it that misinterpreting differences of opinion can be common to so many people? How can a reflex, similar to a knee jerk or an eye blink, be so devastating? In order to answer these questions we need to understand how the habit develops.

Chapter III

In The Beginning

"In all you do or say or think, recollect that at any time the power
of withdrawal from life is in your own hands."
Marcus Aurelius

Humans are frail as compared to other species. We don't possess superior strength, poisons, quills, fangs, wings, or camouflage to help ensure our survival. We rely on intelligence, potentially a much more powerful weapon, to control our environment.

The problem-solving aspect of intelligence has developed over centuries to the point where we can launch rockets into space to explore planets that will eventually become home to the colonies that will settle them. We have developed strong medicines to stamp out horrible diseases and have made the world a smaller place thanks to air travel and the Internet.

Although we are born with the capabilities for contact with the environment and for problem-solving, they must develop over time. How our intelligence develops depends, to a large degree, on our experiences during childhood.

As infants, we are remarkably dependent on those around us for our physical and emotional needs. We not only require food, shelter, and physical safety, but we also need to be loved and to feel secure in our relationships with our families and caretakers. With familiarity, we come to love those who care for us. The last thing on earth we want to do is offend them. We don't want to jeopardize our relationships with those we rely on and who've treated us so well. It is in this protected setting that we come to develop our intelligence, our skills, and our interaction with others outside the family.

Humans are social. We live together, form societies, create rules to help us get along, construct governments on local, state, and federal levels, and elect officials to represent us and to safeguard our welfare. We need to interact with others of our kind. We want to feel accepted, and we suffer greatly if we are somehow isolated from human contact.

The way we learn to cooperate with one another and to live in harmony is through the process of socialization. Socialization refers to the procedure by which a child learns the beliefs and attitudes of his group and internalizes expectations for his behavior. In order to learn acceptable attitudes and behaviors, pressure is exerted for the child to conform.

The methods used to teach our children social values and behaviors are guilt and fear. Sounds terrible but actually the techniques are proper and can be used without hurt or pain to the child. For example, let's say you're five years old. You come home from school one day and tell your mother that you hit another child. Your mother looks at you with hurt on her face and says to you in a sympathetic voice, "But honey, you may have hurt that child." You look at your mother's face, hear her words and you feel bad or guilty. As a result, you don't hit children anymore. If you break the rules at home, at school or at other places, you suffer consequences. Since you don't like the consequences, you don't break the rules anymore.

As you grow, the guilt you feel for hurting others causes you to develop social behaviors such as cooperation, compassion, consideration, camaraderie, tact and so on. Fear of consequences for breaking the law and social mores causes nervousness.

As an adult, you are social and law-abiding so that you don't feel guilt or fear. This condition leaves you free to enjoy life and to get along with others. The key to successful socialization is to have the child learn to cooperate without eliminating spontaneous expression. With this end product, the child grows to an intelligent, contributing member of society who can live life to the fullest.

However, many times parents will use guilt and fear on a child in situations involving differences of opinion. Now, you're five years old and come home from school to find that your mother baked a cake. She says, "Try it. Tell me if you like it." You try a piece and express your taste. "Don't like it, Mom." Your mother looks pained and, in a dejected tone, says, "But I made it for you." Now you've done it. You hurt her. She loves you so much, cleans up after you, washes your clothes, feeds you, tucks you in at night, buys you candy, gives you big hugs, takes you to see Santa and so much more. How could you possibly hurt her like that? And suppose she gets angry at you and stops loving you? What would you do then?

"What's that funny feeling?" You're scared. You know you did something wrong, but what was it and what do you do about it now? You think real fast. "I know. I told mom that I didn't like the cake." Then you say, "Mom, I was only kidding. I really like the cake." You see your mother's face lighten and you know you're safe. Now your mother is smiling while you eat a slice of that awful cake and you think, "Wow! That was close."

Although the child adjusted to the situation, believing that offending mom would result in her anger and rejection, the important lesson to the child is that differences of opinion can be acts that offend, and angry retaliation may follow.

All parents will, at times, use guilt and fear to have a child comply. The technique is not performed maliciously and usually doesn't hurt the child. It's ordinarily used to expedite situations where there are differences of opinion. All children are placed in similar positions and they all come up with the same solution. They hold back expression, anticipate what is expected, and comply. Usually the child comes to understand the point of her parent and adopts the attitude and behavior as logical. This is the meat of the socialization process.

However, suppose a child is placed in situations that require him to hold back expression, to anticipate and comply too frequently? To better understand how the process becomes a habit or reflex, a short psychology history lesson is necessary.

In 1902, while studying digestive reflexes in dogs, Ivan Pavlov noted associations between the dogs' notice of food and salivation. This observation led to his landmark research. Pavlov paired the ringing of a bell with meat powder blown in the dogs' faces. He rang a bell, blew the meat powder and then measured the amount of salivation produced by the dogs. After repeating the procedure a number of times, Pavlov found that the dogs salivated to the sound of the bell alone, without the meat powder. Pavlov was actually able to teach a "<u>born with</u>" or autonomic behavior (salivation) to respond to a previously meaningless event (the sound of the bell).

Pavlov's experiment is important information for us. Suppose we pair expression with fear? Fear is a born with or autonomic response just as salivation is. When we feel fear, our bodies become mobilized against threat. We become ready to fight or run. If a child expresses an opinion or taste and receives criticism, anger or is made to feel guilt in response, the child will eventually feel fear.

Generally, the child's holdback is mild and, although fear is triggered, she may not be consciously aware of either the feeling or the resulting holdback or constriction. However, in situations where she views the difference of opinion as important or of high value, she will be aware of the fear. Whether she is aware of the fear or not, each pairing of expression with criticism indicates that differences are not acceptable. Holding back expression, anticipating what is expected and complying work very well for the child. "Everyone seems to like me." But the cost is heavy. She thinks and thinks, "What is it about me that gets people mad?" It seems that many different people get angry with her, at all different times, for all different behaviors, even when she is doing nothing at all. She doesn't really know, but can figure out when the "bad thing" occurs. "It's when I say what I think or do things the way I want. That's when people seem to get mad at me." What can the child do? Now the body takes over. It attempts to safeguard the child by keeping her out of the place where the "bad thing" may occur, the present. The present is where events occur and where the child should respond spontaneously out of her taste.

If her expression is frequently paired with fear, it will literally take on the negative quality of the fear. The body, for economy, internalizes the process as a <u>habit</u> or reflex. Now the holdback, anticipation and compliance are out of the child's conscious control and occur whenever she is in a situation to express.

Mere existence is expression since we at least have thoughts in the form of attitudes in response to our surroundings. This would mean that RAD is continuously triggered. As a result, whenever the child is in the position (the present) to express an opinion or behave according to her taste, fear is triggered and constriction occurs. The constriction is immediately followed by out-of-control thoughts, and the child is effectively distracted from the environment and spontaneous expression is assassinated.

A few situations to expedite differences of opinion with a child are not enough to build the bad habit so long as the usual interaction with her allows acceptance of her expression. However, if the atmosphere of the communication is intolerance or a lack of acceptance, the ground is fertile for the bad habit to develop.

Many forms of interaction with a child will foster the bad habit. Most obvious is abuse, where the child is forced to comply. Fear of physical assault for the expression of differences with a parent or authority figure soon develops the bad habit feeling of fear and the behavior of constriction. She is made to feel physically inferior, not sure when physical or verbal assault may occur. However, one thing is sure, the child knows that retaliation will come if she expresses an opinion that is unacceptable. Physical, sexual, and psychological abuse all have the same effect in that the child comes to feel inadequate, worthless, insecure and vulnerable, constantly in a state of alarm over threat.

However, the great majority of parents and authority figures are not at all abusive. So how does the habit form in so many people? Let's take some of our patients and look at how the bad habit formed in them.

Sandy and his family came to America from Italy when he was five years old. He quickly took to the English language, and by the age of eight, helped his parents navigate grocery shopping, doctor's appointments, bill payments, interactions with neighbors and all other matters that required translation.

Since his parents never learned English, they became more and more dependent on Sandy's help. As a result, he was quick to be home after school since there was always need for his intervention with some matter important to the family. Although Sandy enjoyed playing with the neighborhood kids, he always felt hesitant to be away from home should his parents need him. He felt anger and resentment toward his parents but guilt at the same time because of their closeness, love and generosity.

By the time he was seventeen, the expression of Sandy's taste was paired with guilt for wanting to do as he liked and fear that somehow his parents would be hurt, with negative consequences to follow. He began having anxiety attacks whenever he went out and during his free time at home. His out-of-control thoughts, attempting to identify the enemy, came up with all kinds of horrible situations to attribute to the badness contained in his taste.

Fear that he had hit someone with his car or had touched a woman inappropriately, despite his knowledge that he had done neither, were attempts to identify the enemy. These thoughts were contrary to his value and moral systems and attested to Sandy's reduced contact with reality and expression of his taste. Compulsions and rituals filled his free time, especially at home, distracting him from the present and eliminating spontaneous expression. Sandy's habit was remarkably efficient in keeping him from expressing. It effectively decreased his awareness of his surroundings by distracting his attention with negative thoughts of the future, of the past and of what people thought of him. As a result, he was anxious and depressed. At times, when Sandy got a break from his anxiety and depression, which was rare, he would sit in front of the TV, dazed off and oblivious. The habit and its sequence were extremely effective in stopping Sandy from enjoying life.

Bill experienced the same sequence of the bad habit as Sandy. Bill felt anxiety and depression, but his major symptom was anger. Like Sandy, Bill tended to take differences of opinion personally. While he held back expression for fear of offending (a condition that generated anxiety, avoidance and depression), he was angry since he interpreted differences from others as criticism. Bill automatically anticipated that people would find fault with him even before they had a chance to say a word.

Bill's problems troubled his family. His parents loved him dearly. Bill was their first-born and he got anything he wanted. His parents always took his side, even if he was wrong. His mother protected him from any potential injury and wouldn't allow him to play too roughly or to take risks that might cause a skinned knee or elbow. His mother and father wouldn't even let Bill remove the training wheels from his bicycle until he was seven and then only after Bill had thrown a temper tantrum because the neighborhood children started calling him a "baby."

Bill's parents also made decisions for him. They didn't want him to make a mistake that he might have to pay for. But Bill knew how to get his way; he would throw temper tantrums. These scenes were horrible. They might occur at any time, at a relative's home, a shopping mall, the doctor's office, anywhere. Bill's parents were embarrassed by their son's behavior but were more concerned over how red his face got. The tantrums always ended the same, his parents gave in and Bill got his way.

His parents overprotected and indulged him out of love. There was no maliciousness or intent to damage their son but when they said, "Here, let me do it for you," Bill heard the words, "Because you can't do it right yourself." Bill grew up feeling somehow "less" than other people. He lacked confidence since he never really had the opportunity to try and handle situations and to learn from his mistakes. He was depressed over not feeling free to try things and to be "himself" and he felt angry over feeling trapped and controlled by his insecurity. He was angry with his parents for their lack of trust in him, but mostly, Bill was angry with himself. He knew there was something wrong with him, but he didn't know what it was. All he knew was when he was in situations that called for a decision, his thoughts would race, his vision got blurry, his heart would pound, and he would feel like a frightened child. Bill didn't know where the feelings came from. He didn't want to tell anyone. They might think he was crazy. He knew he had something "bad" inside him that made him different from other people and he tried to hide it with all his strength.

One way Bill tried to handle his thought that he was less than others was to be physically stronger than they. He started weight lifting around the age of fourteen. He liked to feel strong. By the time he was eighteen, Bill was bulging. He surrounded himself with friends who were just as angry as he was. Bill became intimidating, aggressive, and arrogant. He wasn't going to let anyone put him down. He was ready.

Bill's expression was paired with criticism by the overprotection and overindulgence of his parents. In their effort to show their love, Bill's parents actually punished their son's expression. He experienced decreased attention and awareness whenever he was in situations to express. Almost immediately, out-of-control thoughts would identify the enemy as his inability to handle the situation and would fabricate negative consequences. Then the anxiety would mount. He would avoid expression and his anxiety would reduce. However, the soothing comfort of his avoidance would then generate depression since Bill was not behaving as he wanted. He would feel trapped and controlled by his lack of expression and feel out of control of his life. Frustration and anger would increase and he would explode at anyone whom he believed was critical of him. Bill threw a temper tantrum when faced with out-of-control thoughts about people finding fault with him.

Jenny's parents fought all the time when she was a little girl. Her mother had been hospitalized on two occasions for depression, and her father drank too much. Her father called her mother all sorts of horrible names like "stupid," "crazy" and the worst curse words Jenny had ever heard on the streets of Jersey City. It seemed her father was always angry about something or other. Problems at work, difficulty paying bills, even the Giants' loss to the Cowboys was somehow her mother's fault.

Jenny's mother was helpless. Not only did she allow her husband to abuse her, but she often agreed that his misery was her responsibility. She agonized over where she went wrong but could never figure it out. The woman worried so much that nothing ever got done at home. When she did do something around the house, it would become a compulsion. She might clean the bathroom for hours, annoying her husband who wanted her to get another beer for him while he watched TV. If she cooked, which was rare, she would make so much food that the family couldn't possibly eat it before it turned bad.

Jenny never saw warmth and affection between her parents, only disgust and antagonism. At eleven years old, she knew other parents weren't like hers. She knew that from seeing her friends with their parents at school. Her parents were different. They were unhappy, and for some reason, neither of them was about to change the situation, no matter how bad it was.

With her mother unable to care for the house and the family, and her father only interested in beer and sports, Jenny, as the oldest of three girls, took up the responsibility. She cooked for the family and cleaned the house. She would get up early to see that her sisters were ready for school and walked them to their classrooms before going to her own. Jenny often had to baby-sit her mother through anxiety attacks, depression and ill health while taking criticism from her father for anything that she did, which never seemed to be right. She never really took her father seriously. Even at her young age, Jenny knew her father was simply unhappy and needed to have things wrong to excuse and to justify his foul mood and unhappiness.

Jenny felt sorry for her mother and didn't like seeing her as pathetic, but she did. She didn't really mind caring for her sisters and her parents. She loved them. The problem was that all her duties were more than a child her age was actually capable of managing. Jenny couldn't shake the thought there was something waiting for her that she would not be able to manage. Despite her above age abilities, there existed a frailness within her that would one day hurt her. Jenny didn't know what it was, but she knew it was bad. Then her mother died of cancer. Although she'd often been sick, it was always a cold or fatigue. One day she complained of pain in her back, was admitted to the hospital through the emergency room and passed away within two weeks. Jenny was devastated. Her mother's illness was so invisible, so secret, and so lethal.

Jenny's thoughts began to center around the "bad thing" that she believed was in her. She didn't know whether it was in her mind or her body. She didn't know if it was something that was growing inside her as it had in her mother, or maybe it was something about her mind and what was in her thoughts that would finally hurt her. She became more cautious as she grew older. If she didn't take any chances, maybe the "bad thing" wouldn't happen. Her father's criticism, situations that tested her limits and might well end in failure, and her concern for the "invisible enemy," all led to the pairing of expression with fear. Jenny left her alcoholic father after her sisters were old enough to be on their own. She married a controlling man who was critical of her and made decisions for her so she didn't have to worry.

It is obvious where Jenny's fear of handling money and of the laundry room came from. However, these fears and her strange behaviors were nothing more than avoidant behaviors, functioning only to prevent Jenny from expression so the "bad thing" wouldn't happen. Her expression was paired with criticism from her father, dependency from her mother but mostly from managing situations above her maturational level, thereby ensuring failure, at least in Jenny's mind, where she questioned her performance and felt lucky if she did handle a task. Her out-of-control thoughts attached to all kinds of situations, such as contracting germs from handling money to committing suicide. Although these thoughts were not logical to Jenny, her condition of decreased intelligence had her vulnerable enough to consider the thoughts as real. As a result, she avoided expression by constricting her behavior and remaining in her bedroom. However, Jenny became depressed since she was not experiencing pleasure from behaving as she liked. She felt trapped and controlled by her situation and angry with herself. She was self-critical over her weakness, convincing herself that she was inadequate to change her situation, and therefore reinforcing her lack of expression. Jenny, like the others, experienced the sequence of the bad habit.

Unlike Jenny, Sarah's childhood was wonderful. Her parents were intelligent people who married later in life, and as a result, had Sarah as their only child. Sarah's father was a criminal attorney, and her mother was an English professor. They were upwardly mobile people and always wanted the best for their child. Her parents were not wealthy but comfortable with their two incomes.

Sarah attended the best school in the area and did very well. She was attentive to her homework and would get the highest test grades in her class. She constantly volunteered for extra projects and headed any committee for extra credit.

Sarah was also busy after school. She attended dance classes, took flute lessons, studied acting, and participated in the journalism club. Her parents were very proud of their daughter and her achievements. However, whenever Sarah wanted to engage her taste, such as taking a pottery class or a karate lesson, her parents would discourage such frivolous activities, questioning her as to how the knowledge would advance her culturally and economically. They also discouraged Sarah from playing with the neighborhood children too frequently since she had so much to accomplish in so little time. Sarah remembered always feeling nervous whenever she had free time. She would feel guilty, as if she was doing something wrong.

The message Sarah received as a child was that activity needed to result in accomplishment for it to be acceptable. Clearly, Sarah came to believe her tastes to be bad or wrong. This pairing of her expression with criticism produced fear and developed the habit in Sarah. Her out-of-control thoughts that she would be "bad" if she did as she wanted generated anxiety, especially during free time when Sarah could do as she liked. Her avoidant behaviors of overworking and, in her free time, alcohol abuse, reduced her anxiety since they eliminated spontaneous expression. Sarah experienced depression from her monotonous routine and felt trapped and controlled, with no end in sight. Her anger converted to frustration, self-criticism and guilt for feelings of dissatisfaction with the life that her parents had spent so much time and money to help her build. The sequence of the habit, as with the other patients, reinforced Sarah's self-critical thoughts that she must avoid spontaneous expression since there was something "bad" contained within her taste.

Fran's parents also loved her very much. However, Fran's mother was very controlling. Her father was passive and allowed his wife her way rather than trying to outtalk her. Fran felt the same. Her mother was relentless so that Fran submitted to her mother's point of view rather than hear a lecture on how her mother had more experience in these matters. It wasn't that her mother would yell or go into a tirade; she simply persisted and was always right, while Fran was always wrong.

As a result, Fran lacked confidence. She couldn't make decisions and would never say "no" to anyone. She felt men only tolerated her and saw herself as less desirable than other women. She questioned her own thoughts and felt out-of-control of everything. The only thing Fran felt she could control was her weight.

Fran's expression was paired with criticism by a relentless mother. Although her mother often declared that she was only appealing to her daughter's intelligence, Fran always detected anger beneath her mother's words and her artificial smile. Fran knew she should stand up for herself once she reached adolescence, but her early childhood of expression paired with the criticism of her mother's control proved too strong a habit for Fran's intelligence to fight off.

Fran was always uncomfortable, waiting for the "bad thing" to happen. In situations to express, her habit would attach to some fabricated event and Fran would experience panic attacks that she endured for hours. Although Fran emphasized her weight as the only behavior she could control, her gorging and purging was nothing more than an avoidant behavior that occupied her time and eliminated expression. Avoidance kept her anxiety down to a mild discomfort, but Fran was depressed over her nowhere life. She felt angry that she couldn't change her personality and find a worthwhile relationship away from her mother and her obsession with her weight. She turned her anger inward, critical of her worthlessness and inability to be more expressive, like her mother. Fran knew that she would continue to hold back her expression since nothing good could possibly result from it.

Jerry, too, came from a good family. There was affection and communication between his parents and they showed him much love and attention. However, when Jerry's brother, Robert, was born, he had to share their attention. It became worse when Robert developed some kind of a fever that threatened his life. His parents seemed to put Jerry aside and pay particular attention to Robert. Jerry felt guilty for resenting his brother and tried to make up for it by being especially good. He cleaned his room, ran to get Robert's medication, got his father's slippers, and helped in any way that he could.

It wasn't so much that his parents ignored him. They still spent quality time with Jerry. They simply had to attend to Robert's health. Jerry understood this but couldn't stop the holdback. He became more and more constricted as he got older. He wasn't unhappy, he just wasn't fully spontaneous, conforming to expectations and missing out on the enjoyment of life.

At first glance, it might be difficult to see how Jerry's expression was paired with criticism. His parents appeared to be loving and expressive with Jerry, despite Robert's illness. The habit didn't result in severe symptoms as in some of the others, but it did stop Jerry from living to the fullest.

He didn't receive criticism that we can see. Jerry's criticism for his expression came from within. It was Jerry's own thoughts that had him believe he was unworthy of his parent's attention. As a result, he held back expression, anticipated what was expected and complied. Although Jerry felt depressed and angry over the situation, he also felt guilt for his feelings. He saw his need for attention to be selfish, and he continued to hold back expression for fear of hurting the ones whom he loved and stimulating their anger toward him.

It was Jerry's own misinterpretation of the situation concerning his parents and Robert that paired his expression with criticism. Jerry believed he was somehow unacceptable to his parents and became concerned over their attention toward Robert. He anticipated what his parents expected and complied. His avoidant behaviors reduced the anxiety that his parents may no longer care for him. When he anticipated their wants he was needed, or at least tolerated.

However, the pairing of Jerry's expression with his negative misinterpretations developed the habit as surely as if he had been a victim of abuse. While not as intense as many of the others, the habit existed in Jerry just as surely and functioned to stop him from living fully.

As an adult, Jerry wouldn't take chances, even in situations where risk was minimal. He lived a conservative lifestyle, careful not to make waves. His constriction and reluctance to experience differences and changes made him a model citizen so society would not have to be concerned that Jerry might break the rules. Jerry was concerned over breaking rules that simply didn't exist. As a result, he missed out on much of the flavor and excitement of life.

Jerry's case demonstrates the misperception that is common among children. An unintentional glance away, a smile, laughing at something cute that a child may do, may all be misinterpreted by the child. Even though these situations occur frequently and do not result in the development of the habit in many children, Jerry's situation was somewhat special. Robert's condition made it easier for Jerry's misperception to occur. Jerry's misinterpretations occurred frequently. As an adult, Jerry continues to do the "right thing" even though it would not break any rules if he did as he liked. Jerry continues to be a 35-year-old "good boy."

Unlike previous cases, Bob's expression was accepted and encouraged by his parents when he was a child. Differences of opinion were viewed as points of view. Guilt and fear were used appropriately and Bob was not forced to comply with his parents' opinions. He was allowed to express, offered an alternative but encouraged to make his own choice, with support for any outcome.

Bob didn't develop the habit during childhood. He experienced normal nervousness in valued social situations and disappointment when certain things didn't go his way, but not anxiety or depression. So where did his symptoms come from? Clearly, he experienced out-of-control thoughts, anxiety, sleep problems and more after his auto accident.

In Bob's case, the habit developed instantly as a result of the accident. The impact impressed Bob's mind and body with the information that harm may occur "out of the blue" and without warning. The intense fear that he experienced was sufficient to develop the bad habit in a "one-shot" learning. The fight-flight response was triggered as a result of the event and continued chronically because of the perceived inability to prevent a recurrence of the same or similar event that could jeopardize Bob's health and life. The lack of information concerning a recurrence fed out-of-control, negative thoughts and generalized to all kinds of situations so Bob didn't feel safe anywhere.

As in Bob's case, I once saw a woman who developed the habit after an auto accident. As a result, she refused to leave her home because something could happen. Soon after, she developed anxiety at home, since an airplane could crash into her house. Finally, she began to have anxiety over the thought that she could have a heart attack at any moment. The lack of information concerning discomfort from decreased attention, spiraled into all kinds of fabrications, regardless of the probability in reality, and resulted in severe anxiety for both Bob and my female patient.

The situations above, while different in content, all contain the same element. In each case, as a child, expression was paired with fear. However, in Bob's case the habit developed from one dramatic situation where expression was paired with intense fear.

If expression is met with what the child sees as criticism, fear will be induced. With sufficient repetition, expression takes on the negative quality of the fear and evolves into a style that affects all the child's thinking and behavior. Since the child can't figure out what expression will meet with anger and produce negative consequences, the habit reduces all the child's contact with the environment so that spontaneous expression cannot occur. Most important, the sequence of symptoms that follows when the habit is triggered is the same for all individuals. The content of the thoughts and behaviors experienced as symptoms are irrelevant, except in cases where the individual's health and welfare or that of another person is jeopardized. The function of the symptoms is always the same: to prevent spontaneous expression by distracting the individual from events in the environment.

While the influence of the habit is constant, the discomfort generated may not always be experienced. The discomfort may maintain at a low intensity and you may become accustomed to the feeling and believe it to be ordinary and part of your general personality make-up. The habit is continually reducing awareness, a condition that produces mild tension. The habit thought, that something bad will happen, seeks to attach to any valued situation in order to justify the discomfort and to identify the occurrence of the "bad thing."

This is why those with the habit tend to find fault with themselves. Some may think that they're too short, too tall, too thin, too heavy, not smart enough, etc. Even if the person is able to rectify the complaint, some other shortcoming will be used to identify the enemy. This negative style of thinking usually follows the child throughout her life, robbing her of spontaneity, expression of taste, and happiness.

While the quality of the child's interaction with his parents and primary caretakers is the most important element in the development of the habit, the process of holdback is frequently reinforced by situations and individuals outside the family.

Authority figures, teachers, clergy, coaches, and others may use anger and guilt to force compliance and expedite situations involving differences of opinion. For instance, an overzealous teacher may use anger to make a child comply. I recall my grade school days in the times when corporal punishment was acceptable and common. If a child's homework wasn't correct, or if she didn't understand her lessons, she might be whacked on the knuckles with a ruler or a pointer. Sometimes she was made to feel embarrassment or humiliation. Fear of negative consequences forced holdback, anticipation of what was expected, and compliance.

I also recall my baseball coach criticizing me for "hanging out" with my friends on some evenings. He believed that my interest in baseball was compromised by my social interaction with my friends. Interestingly, my performance on the field suffered after our conversations. However, I believe the errors I made were not the result of my social interest, but of my divided attention. I felt the coach always had his eyes on me, waiting for me to make a mistake.

It is common knowledge that friends and peers can exert a tremendous influence on a child. A child wants to be accepted and part of the group. Teasing, taunting and criticism can sometimes be vicious among children. Some children from a particularly critical family may seek acceptance from a peer group and identify with the group's negative behaviors and values in order to gain acceptance. It is quite common for children to hold back expression, anticipate what is expected, and comply in order to be a part of a peer group.

Even the media may discourage differences of opinion. For instance, a commercial may suggest that if a child doesn't wear a certain brand of jeans, he may risk being identified as a nerd. The same pressure is so for toys or other items. Throughout history, marketing influences has been responsible for some extremely successful sales campaigns.

Usually no one situation or incident is responsible for the development of the bad habit in a child. More important is the atmosphere in which the child is raised. If the attitude in the home and between parents and children is one of open communication with acceptance of expression and with differences viewed as points of view rather than as angry acts that offend, the child is less likely to develop the bad habit and to be influenced by criticism outside the family.

From the above discussion, it may appear that the habit is so all encompassing that a remedy seems impossible. If you were to see a doctor to stop your anxiety, would she need to address each and every situation where you feel nervous? Is it possible that one technique could change how you look at all situations at once? If you weren't to lose awareness, might that mean you wouldn't feel nervous? Such a technique would certainly be an advance for those who suffer the pain of psychological discomfort. One technique for all psychological discomfort would oppose the current thinking that different disorders are caused by different sources and therefore in need of different treatments. How could it be that all the past scientific research could have missed a single cause for symptoms and a standard technique to eliminate them? Maybe the technique is too simple and easily missed in a society that believes if you can't make it big, paint it red.

Chapter IV

Attention Training

Back in 1988, my patients and I would fight the habit. I had long realized the major problem for my patients was decreased awareness of the environment. Decreased awareness could only occur if they somehow became inattentive. I could see that with decreased awareness of the world, their perception was inaccurate and their <u>symptoms</u> resulted from negative thoughts that had little or nothing to do with reality. But how could I have my patients increase their attention, and would they really feel better, or was the current medical thinking that a genetic problem or a biochemical imbalance is responsible for their discomfort really correct? If so, why was I seeing these people? Simply to hold their hands and to sympathize with the hopelessness of their situations?

I was ready for something, for the next step in my ideas concerning decreased attention. It was during this frustration that I met Sandy, one of my most difficult cases and one who, because of his horrible symptoms, pushed me to work harder to develop my theory and an effective <u>treatment</u> technique.

Sandy was a sweet man who had seen approximately twelve psychiatrists and psychologists before he came to me. The doctors had tried all kinds of medications, searched his past for problems, used behavior modification and, finally, all gave up. It wasn't that Sandy hadn't been cooperative. He wanted to feel better. He stuck it out with each of them, sometimes for years. Sandy was motivated, willing and hurting. The truth was that the doctors simply didn't know what to do with him. No matter what technique they tried, they were doing exactly what Sandy did, trying to identify the enemy. All their science was reduced to guess work. In the final analysis, none of it was effective.

Sandy made his first appointment with me some time in November of 1988. The weather was harsh and Sandy was especially cold as a result of his walk from the bus stop to my office. Sandy was soft-spoken, extremely polite and appeared to be meek. He related his terrible compulsions, rituals, and thoughts to me. His eyes were glazed and he appeared to be desperate.

I explained my theory to Sandy, and he thought it too simple to be true but admitted that it did explain what he felt and why he behaved as he did. Sandy, like so many other patients, and even doctors, mistakenly believed that serious symptoms must result from serious causes. As with my other patients, I asked Sandy to pamper himself, to treat himself well. I asked him to take long baths, play music he liked, light candles, turn off the phone, and enjoy walks. I believed that if Sandy felt stimulation from the world, his attention would be more focused on his surroundings and less on his disturbing thoughts.

These first attempts to have my patients increase attention were quite crude. I remember having Sandy watch his hand as he turned Christmas bulbs into their sockets on the large tree in his front yard. All the time, Sandy and I battled the illogic of his habit. Fighting the habit was like counterpunching. The habit would hit Sandy, and we would knock down the thoughts and symptoms while we tried to push Sandy's attention out toward the environment where it belonged. It was painstaking work.

Sandy made some progress and he was thankful. However, I wasn't satisfied at all. I knew his progress wasn't sufficient to warrant the time and energy we had spent knocking down his illogical thoughts and symptoms. I knew then that it was useless for Sandy and me to battle the habit. As much as I tried, I couldn't get his intelligence in front of the habit to prevent its occurrence. It was too fast. As soon as it was there, it was everywhere and Sandy couldn't get out of it. If we fought off one thought or symptom, another would appear to take the place of the first.

When the habit was triggered with intensity, it was instantaneous and all encompassing. Sandy described it as similar to a light switch thrown off and on. When the switch was thrown, the light was everywhere, when off, nothing but darkness. The other problem was that when Sandy's intelligence was decreased, it didn't have the strength to fight the bad habit effectively. The thoughts seemed to come from out of nowhere and might concern anything, no matter how incredible or bizarre. It was like standing in a room with the lights out while a silent antagonizer poked him with a stick and his attempts to grab the stick were always a bit too slow. The situation made Sandy feel vulnerable, inadequate and always at the will of the bad habit.

It was some time into Sandy's treatment when it occurred to me that, since a reflex or habit occurs so fast as to not be controlled, then don't try to control it. Completely ignore it and put all the patient's energy into building a new habit to counteract the bad one. But how could we build a new habit that had the strength to keep a person focused and, at the same time, fend off the thoughts and symptoms of the bad habit?

I understood the bad habit developed by pairing expression with fear. In order to build a new habit, I could use the same pairing process to increase the patient's intelligence. But which aspect of intelligence would I use? Logic, memory, problem-solving, there were so many aspects of intelligence to choose from that finding the right one was going to be a problem.

I knew the bad habit had a sequence. Decreased awareness was the result of reduced attention toward the environment. The decreased awareness caused discomfort. Attention was converted to out-of-control thoughts to justify the discomfort and to quell confusion. These thoughts triggered anxiety with its intensity determined by the value of the situation and the lack of knowledge of the behavior required. To reduce anxiety, expression was avoided and depression was generated since pleasure could not be produced. This led to a feeling of being trapped and controlled by a miserable existence that caused anger to be acted out, with guilt and self-criticism to follow, completing a cycle that repeated itself. I knew this sequence worked like a machine in the same way for all people.

It seemed logical to me that if I reversed the sequence, I should be able to decide what aspect of the process took place first. The guilt and self-criticism occurred in response to unwarranted anger, which was triggered by feeling trapped and controlled by depression. Depression was generated by avoidance of expression that is used to reduce anxiety. The anxiety resulted from the out-of-control thoughts, with its intensity determined by the value placed on the situation and the lack of <u>familiarity</u> with the necessary behavior. The out-of-control thoughts and the decreased awareness of the environment resulted from reduced attention or focus.

There it was. If I could prevent a patient from losing attention or <u>focus</u> toward the environment, symptoms could not occur since the sequence of the habit could not be triggered. But how to do it? Simply instructing Sandy and the others to be more attentive didn't seem to work. They all said they were attentive. I needed to be specific and to decide what to pair attention with. I knew contact with the environment in the present was natural so increased attention would automatically be pleasurable. In psychology, there is a well-known and understood theory called the <u>Pleasure Principle</u>. This means that if an organism (in this case the human body) is presented with conditions of pleasure and pain, pleasure will be chosen every time. I believed if I paired my patient's increased attention toward the environment with pleasure, with repetition a new reflex or habit could be formed that would cancel out the effects of the bad habit. All I needed were the tools.

I needed to devise a way to have Sandy and my other patients train their bodies to be more attentive and focused toward the environment. If such a reflexive tendency could be attained, then awareness would be automatic and symptoms could not be generated.

The technique of <u>Attention Training</u> is intended to build a <u>new habit</u> of increased awareness by pairing attention directed toward the environment with pleasure. I believed a new habit could be built in the body with the conscious, deliberate intention of my patients. In devising a method to have my patients increase awareness, I realized I needed to be very specific in detailing the procedure. I needed to be clear so my patients could obtain the outcome we wanted as quickly as possible.

The <u>Four Points</u> to build the new habit became the tools Sandy and the others needed to reduce their symptoms by increasing attention, and therefore, awareness of the environment. The Four Points are:

1. *Deliberately <u>orient</u> yourself to time and place.* Consciously know where you are and what's going on around you. Right now, I know I'm at home, in Belmar. I know that it's Saturday night at 11:42 p.m., and I'm typing on my computer. I know it's January 8, 2000 and the temperature outside is around 37 degrees and the stereo is playing music on random.

2. *Use one or more of the five senses.* Consciously see, hear, smell, touch, and taste. The easiest and most used senses are seeing, hearing, and feeling. I can hear the background music as I type, as well as the sound of the keys as I touch them. I can see my fingers move and see the words on the screen. I can feel that it's a little warm in the house, and I can feel my knee leaning on the desk leg. If I was outside, walking the boardwalk, I could feel the coolness and the wind. I could see the moon and the clouds. I could hear the sound of the ocean waves hitting the shore and the sound of the traffic on Ocean Avenue, and I could smell the salt air. If I was watching TV, I would consciously and deliberately watch the figures move on the screen and hear the sound that played along with the picture.

3. *Be active, don't <u>drift</u>, daydream, or <u>daze off</u>.* <u>Activity</u> is any voluntary behavior. Walking, talking to a friend on the

phone, watching TV, listening to music, writing, or virtually any other behavior that you decide to do is an activity. The key is to do the activity consciously and deliberately. If you find yourself drifting in front of the TV or anywhere else, break it with activity. Get up and get a drink of water or call a friend, anything.

4. *Only think or have on your mind what is hitting your senses.* In other words, if you can't see, hear, smell, touch, or taste it, it doesn't exist. Don't think it, it will probably be negative and cause symptoms. What should be on your mind is what's happening right now, at this moment, <u>in front of you</u>, in the present.

The idea of the Four Points is to be concrete in your thinking. If you can't see hear, smell, touch or taste it, don't think it.

––––––––––

Sounds simple, but the Four Points is actually quite hard to perform, at least in the beginning. How difficult each is to execute depends on how much <u>resistance</u> a person experiences from the bad habit. The resistance occurs because the body wants to behave as it has learned. For instance, let's say you write with your right hand and want to learn to write with your left as well. In order to accomplish the task, you would have to be very conscious to remember to pick up the pen with your left hand and deliberately write the letters you wish. However, if you forget to use your left hand the next time you write, you will automatically pick up the pen with your right hand and place it to the paper. The body always goes back to what it knows. It does this for economy. The same is true with the Four Points.

_____

Resistance to the Four Points will occur in five ways which Sandy, my patients and anyone with the habit will encounter:

1. *You will forget to do the Four Points.* The hardest task concerning the Four Points is to remember to do them. Amazingly, with the slightest distraction, the Four Points will be out of your mind, and the body will return to the holdback of the habit. To help with this problem, I asked Sandy to make copies of the Points and to keep them everywhere. I asked him to keep them on the bathroom mirror, the nightstand, in his desk at work, a copy in his pocket, and if he was able to drive, in the car. It wasn't so important he read the paper; just seeing it would remind him to be focused. Anything you can do to remember to focus will help develop the new habit sooner.

2. *The thought from the habit will convince you, "I'm too busy, I don't have time to do the Four Points."* I'm doing them as I write, at this moment. It isn't that you must stop what you're doing, focus out and then return to your task. What you want is to behave in a focused manner. The idea is to create a style of attentive contact with the environment.

3. *"I'm home (or in another familiar situation), I don't need to do the Four Points."* The habit is a reflex; it has no intelligence and cannot know where you are. Its intention is only to prevent spontaneous expression. Most people don't experience anxiety at home. They feel relieved they don't need to behave as they do during the day at work, outside or among people. At home or in some other familiar place, avoidance is a dominant symptom since expression is not required, as it is in some other situations. You are unlikely to experience anxiety in familiar places. As a result, it will

be easier to accomplish the Four Points without intense resistance.

4. *"I feel good, I don't need to do the Four Points."* How good you feel at any time may be determined by the distance between your attention level and the habit. Imagine the habit to be at a constant level and your attention toward your surroundings vacillating from sharp focus to dull contact. The sharper your focus, the more distance from the habit, the less intense your symptoms. However, as your attention and focus recede from the environment and become dull, the closer they approach the influence of the habit, and symptoms will be more intense. It is best to attempt the Four Points when your attention level is a good distance from the habit. In this condition you will not only feel comfortable, but with increased attention, you will be able to learn the Four Points with greater ease.

5. *"This theory is too simple, it can't possibly work."* Reflexive Attention Diversion and the intervention of Attention Training are accurate. The sequence of the habit is the same for all people with psychological symptoms. By developing a competing reflex of increased awareness, symptoms can be reduced.

The fifth resistance is actually quite important. That Reflexive Attention Diversion and Attention Training are too simple to explain the complexity of symptoms comes from the confusion and lack of knowledge concerning symptoms, their cause, and how to treat them. Because they appear to be complex, it seems logical that their cause should be equally complex.

Let's take an example. Suppose we wanted to fire two rockets. One is aimed at a specific target on the moon and the other at a target on Pluto. We calculate all the factors necessary to have a successful launch, with one exception. We are slightly off in our calculations to precisely hit our targets on both planets.

The result of our mistake is that we missed our target on the moon by a considerable distance. However, because of the difference in distance from the earth to the moon, our closest relative, and the earth to Pluto, the farthest planet in our solar system, our miss at the target on Pluto was extreme as compared to our miss on the moon. Although our calculations were off only slightly for both targets, the effect was quite different for both our targets. The same is true for RAD and Attention Training. Severe symptoms are, in fact, due to a simple cause.

RAD, like our rocket experiment, maintains that the same cause can be traced to all symptoms. Panic attacks, depression, anger responses, obsessive-compulsive disorder, manic-depression, and all other symptoms, if they are psychological, may be traced to a reflexive decrease in awareness. Attention Training, through the Four Points, is directed specifically at the cause of symptoms and to their elimination in the most efficient manner.

Although it seems logical that extreme symptoms would result from extreme causes, logic has not been able to answer the questions pertaining to the development of symptoms that would lead to treatments for their elimination. Because current theories concerning symptoms are popular, this popularity does not make them accurate. It was once commonly thought and held to be true that the world was flat and that the sun revolved around the earth.

Despite his belief that decreased awareness was too simple an explanation for his severe symptoms, Sandy agreed to try the Four Points. I asked him to perform them as frequently as possible. I told him he should not expect a dramatic change in the beginning since the bad habit would resist the behavioral change of the Four Points. Sandy's job was to consciously and deliberately increase his attention by focusing on the environment using the Points and to notice that, for the brief period of time his attention increased, he felt slightly better. I didn't expect Sandy would feel pleasure; his attention was too diverted from the environment.

What I expected was that Sandy would feel some relief and be a little bit clearer in his mind since his problem could be viewed as a tendency to think too much outside of the here and now. It wasn't deliberate. He couldn't help it. It was reflexive, a bad habit. If he displaced some of the attention that was focused on events outside the present and placed it back on his surroundings where it belonged, he should feel some relief. In addition, if less attention was placed on fabricated negative events, his symptoms should reduce. I couldn't wait for Sandy's next session.

Sandy came to his next session with a half smile on his face. It had worked but had been a battle. Sandy did feel relief, and his symptoms did reduce somewhat. He was able to consciously perform the Four Points. But when he became more focused, and therefore more capable of expression, he got pulled back inside his head and experienced anxiety, which was what I had expected. Sandy was encouraged and agreed that he felt more in control of his symptoms than ever before.

The key to building a new habit in the body is repetition. It wasn't important how long Sandy maintained his increased attention when doing the Four Points. What was important was how frequently he performed them. Take teaching a dog to sit. If you command the dog to sit, and he sits all day, the dog only associates your command with the behavior, to sit, one time. Clearly, one experience is not frequent enough for the dog to learn to sit on command. However, if you repeat the command, have the dog stand then sit and reward him frequently, the probability is that the dog will learn to sit on command sooner. The same is true for learning the new habit. The more frequently the Four Points are performed, the sooner the new habit will be learned.

I instructed my other patients to perform the procedure and got the same results. Regardless of the differences in their backgrounds, symptoms, or current situations, they all improved. I knew I was onto something.

My patients' improvement was extremely significant. It meant there existed a process at work beneath the situational and content differences that produced symptoms. This process was the same for all individuals with symptoms and worked in the same sequence. It also meant I was not treating these individuals, I was teaching them a different style of thinking and perceiving the world. These people weren't sick or ill. Their symptoms were the result of a bad habit, a mislearning or faulty belief system founded on the misinformation that differences of opinion were offensive, angry acts that hurt others and would result in retaliation, and that differences of opinion from others were actually criticism. The association between expression and fear of offending was so frequent that it was quickly learned and now, with the information in the form of the words and deeds that produced them long gone, these individuals were left only with the reflex or habit of holdback and their other symptoms.

I knew some people did have a genetic or biochemical imbalance that produced disorders, but not all of them, or even most of them. Here was an <u>intervention</u> that could be used for the large majority of individuals who experienced symptoms.

The implications were tremendous. Finally, my ideas concerning the connection between decreased awareness and symptoms appeared to be correct. I worked to find as many techniques as I could to have Sandy and the others understand the habit and how it worked.

One of the most important aspects of the habit and how it worked was the thoughts it used to trigger symptoms. I instructed Sandy and the others about their "enemy," out-of-control thinking. Although some out-of-control thoughts have words and pictures attached to them, most are simply attitudes, an apprehension that something bad will happen.

Sandy and the others were asked to monitor their thoughts and to reduce out-of-control thinking by using intelligent answers to the thoughts. The out-of-control thoughts and the intelligent answers to them were given to all my patients:

1. *Future Thinking* occurs when you anticipate an event negatively. Future thinking stimulates anxiety. If you should find you are future thinking say to yourself, with your intelligence, "If I can't see, hear, smell, touch or taste it, it doesn't exist. I'll handle it if it happens or when it's in my face. I'm not going to worry about it now."

2. <u>*Past Thinking*</u> causes depression and relates to a past event that somehow affects the present and future in a negative manner. If you find yourself dwelling in the past, say to yourself, with your intelligence, "It's over. There's nothing I can do about it. I'll stay in the present."

3. <u>*Mind Reading*</u> occurs when you anticipate the thoughts of others in a negative fashion. Mind Reading generates anxiety. You should answer, with your intelligence, "If it doesn't come out of their mouths and off their lips, they're not thinking it."

4. <u>*Avoidant Thinking*</u> or dazing off causes depression. Avoidant thinking occurs when there is decreased activity and events which would engage attention toward the environment. For instance, say you're in front of the TV, watching a program and fifteen minutes later you realize that you've missed a portion of the show and don't know where the time went. Your attention slowly receded. Literally, your senses decreased. Your ability to see, hear, smell, touch, and taste lessened. Other intellectual functions also decreased. You were less oriented, your ability to recognize where you were, what you were doing, the time of day and what was going on around you reduced. Less stimulation reached your senses so that you could not experience pleasure. This lack of stimulation and pleasure to the senses generates depression since you can't enjoy yourself because you're incapable of witnessing events. Avoidant thinking is difficult to prevent. Usually, you notice drifting once you are in it for a while. Break avoidant thinking with activity. Get a glass of water, call a friend, stick your head out the window. Any activity can break drifting. Also, try to identify the situations and times when you tend to drift and enter those situations as focused as possible and maintain your focus for as long as you can. Another

common time when drifting occurs is while you are driving. Consciously notice the cars around you, see the landscape, look at the sky, hear the music from your radio, open your window a little and feel the breeze. If you are performing the Four Points, your tendency to out-of-control think will be decreased.

As can be seen, activity is quite important. However, some activities are better for our purposes than others. Activity that requires participation and holds interest is always the best. Taking a walk, riding a bike and speaking on the phone, all require your participation. In that way, help you to focus outside of your thoughts.

Attention is necessary to perform <u>active activities</u>. You must pay attention when riding a bike or you may crash. If you're speaking on the phone, you must listen to the voice on the other side in order to carry on the conversation. If you are walking, you must attend to where you're going or you might possibly walk into a tree. However, it is more difficult to maintain attention and focus during <u>passive activities</u>. Reading a book or watching TV lend themselves to avoidant thinking or drifting since they don't require sufficient participation. These passive activities, and others, are often performed automatically and with low to no awareness by a person with the bad habit.

The objective of the Four Points is to create a new habit of awareness by pairing increased attention with pleasure. However, the bad habit can't be replaced by the new one. You must build the new habit to a point of sufficient strength so it will not allow the bad one to be triggered. Until the new habit is firmly established, the symptoms of the bad habit will be experienced. However, its symptoms will decrease in intensity over time. The effects of the bad habit taper off as the effects of the new one increase.

It is also important to understand that the Four Points is not designed to get you out of trouble or out of your head once the bad habit is triggered with intensity. The Four Points is designed only to build the new habit. If you get pulled inside your head, use activity.

Sometimes, if you're deep inside, you may need much activity, such as going for a walk, then calling a friend, then going to the mall, then getting a really entertaining video, etc. If you're doing the Four Points consciously, before you are pulled inside your head, chances are you won't be pulled in at all.

The new behaviors and the old habit oppose each other. The brain can't accommodate two requests for opposite behaviors at the same time. You can't be focused and in your head at the same time. Because the body has used the bad habit for so many years, its pathway to the brain is quite efficient and economical. On the other hand, the Four Points is rather new and requires intentional behavior, making its employment cumbersome and awkward in comparison to the bad habit. In a foot race to the brain, the bad habit will arrive first every time. You would need to spend the majority of your time battling to get out of your head, as Sandy initially did. The solution is really quite simple. If you perform the Four Points before you go inside your head with any intensity, you will have the new behaviors in the brain and operating first, before the bad habit can pull you in. The Four Points is intended to build the new habit, not to get you out of trouble. When in trouble, use activity to do most of the work for you.

Some of my patients had trouble understanding that the Four Points was to be used to build the new habit and continued to use it to get out of trouble. I believe their difficulty was not so much with understanding the function of the Four Points but more the result of forgetting to perform it, only remembering to be focused once they found that their attention had decreased and they were once again experiencing symptoms with intensity. Remember to perform the Four Points any way you can.

Another difficulty that Sandy and some others had was the ability to think only of what was happening in the current. "How can you only think in the current? Don't you have to plan ahead?" And, of course, they were right. I realized these were intelligent people, but they had the bad habit influencing their thinking. I couldn't be inside their heads to inform them which thought was intelligent and which one was out-of-control, and I couldn't trust that they could make the determination on their own, they were all too new to the technique. I asked them all to shut down assumption making and past thinking as much as they could. If we could control their thoughts and limit their thinking to the present, we could best assure winding up, as efficiently as possible, with the product we want: intelligent thinking.

However, I thought it important to offer them some information on the kinds and characteristics of intelligent thoughts and habit thoughts so they would have adequate knowledge when confronted with each.

The types of intelligent thought that function outside the present environment include planning, memory, and reminiscing.

1. *Planning*
    A. Planning thoughts focus on a future event.
    B. There is a firm basis for the thought in reality.
    C. A decision is made.
    D. Thinking returns to the present environment without resistance.

2. *Memory*
    A. Memory focuses on a past event(s) with the same or similar theme(s) as the present situation.
    B. A decision is made concerning the past event(s) and its (their) impact on a current or future situation.
    C. Thinking returns to your surroundings without resistance.

3. *Reminiscing*
    A. Reminiscing focuses on a past event(s).
    B. The thoughts are pleasurable.
    C. Thinking returns to the present environment without resistance.

There is only one habit thought, out-of-control, with four varieties: future, past, mind reading and avoidant thinking.

The characteristics of out-of-control thoughts are:

A. Thinking recedes from the environment and focuses on the future, the past, the thoughts of others or on a dullness, void of content (with avoidant thinking B, C, D do not occur).

B. There is no firm basis for the thought in the present or in your surroundings.

C. As a result of the uncertainty resulting from out-of-control thinking, a decision cannot be made.

D. The thinking is self-critical and involved in personal content in order to create value.

E. The habit resists a return to the present.

However, the easiest way to distinguish intelligent thinking from habit or out-of-control thinking is that intelligent thinking is always positive and out-of-control thinking is always negative. Intelligent thinking has one function, to solve problems for your benefit, while habit thinking possesses the sole purpose of preventing expression.

For example, let's say you have next week off from work. You think about it and decide you would like to visit Key West. You've stayed at Jabour's, you like the owner, and it's close to Duval Street. You make the reservations and you're set.

In this decision there is a basis in reality, you have next week off. You go to the future, plan to visit Key West. You even use some memory; you liked Jabour's and remember that it's close to Duval Street. You make your reservations and return to the present.

Now for out-of-control thinking: You've made your decision and you can't wait. Now you start thinking, "Yeah, I deserve this. It's been so long since I've had some time off. But wait. Suppose I don't feel comfortable on the street? I hope people can't tell I'm a tourist. And what if I feel awkward? Will people see that? What will they think of me? I know I've felt awkward in the past. What if...I don't know what, but I know it will be bad. Maybe I'll cancel and stay home. I could get all that work done that I've been putting off."

The out-of-control thoughts did not have any anchor in reality since, at the time you had the thoughts, you weren't actually in Key West on the street with people around you. No decision could be made to handle the problem since the problem was fabricated and outside of the present and because the thoughts spiraled into a vague attitude, void of any structure, "I don't know what, but it will be bad."

The out-of-control thoughts triggered anxiety and you avoided doing what you wanted and were forced to stay home. Although the anxiety reduces as a result of avoidance, you're not doing what you want and depression follows along with the rest of the habit sequence.

Intelligence always functions to solve problems for your benefit and pleasure. Even in a difficult situation, intelligence is working to solve problems. Let's say you worked late and you're walking to your car. You see some menacing looking characters sitting on a bench up ahead and you're concerned. You're nervous and you decide, "If any of them gets up, I'm running into that store over there." Even in "tight" situations, intelligence is working to solve problems for your benefit.

Another point to keep in mind is that intelligent decisions offer you a choice; you can do this or that. Intelligent decisions reflect your taste. However, with decisions influenced by the bad habit there is no choice. You are forced to avoid doing as you want. The bad habit is based on the misinformation that an individual's taste contains an unknown "bad" quality that will result in negative consequences.

Sandy and the other patients were delighted. They understood the concept and all progressed. Some progressed faster than others, but all progressed. I was excited. All my intervention was directed toward Attention Training. As time went on, I spent less and less time on situations, background and symptoms to the point where if the individual was of no physical danger to himself or others, I didn't discuss anything but the bad habit and Attention Training. I found background information wasn't very important and had nothing to do with the patient's problem, except perhaps, for how the habit was developed.

Attention Training proved to be an effective intervention for all sorts of symptoms, and my patients were progressing rapidly. Now, I turned all my attention toward developing techniques to support the Four Points and having my patients maintain contact with the present.

However, I realized I could not use the Four Points with children who had the bad habit. Their intelligence simply wouldn't be at the developmental stage needed to have them understand the concepts of RAD and Attention Training. I also understood that the bad habit appeared responsible for relationship problems. It was after my confidence was stronger with Attention Training for individuals that I began to think of how the concepts of the intervention could be adjusted for children and for relationships.

Chapter V

Toward An Efficient New Habit

"Give your heart to the trade you have learnt, and draw refreshment from it. Let the rest of your days be spent as one who has whole-heartedly committed his all to the gods and is henceforth no man's master or slave."
Marcus Aurelius

Attention Training was working well with every one of my patients. Those with all sorts of symptoms were understanding the theory of the bad habit, performing the Four Points and improving. I was quite satisfied with the intervention and its results.

However, I found there were certain conditions and concepts my patients also needed to know so learning the new habit could be accomplished quicker. If I could have them understand that the holdback of the bad habit is a constant style, which influences them twenty-four hours a day, and in all situations, they might also understand that the expressive style of the new habit would operate in the same way. The more information I could give them, the faster they would be able to build the new habit to resist the bad one and prevent the loss of attention, which caused symptoms.

I needed to make the concept of awareness a bit more concrete, more touchable. I wanted to convert the Four Points into situations and conditions which my patients could equate with awareness and being in control. By the end of 1992, I had developed a number of techniques and concepts to help them understand the bad and the new habits better. The idea was to have them see Attention Training as a real style of thinking and living that could be put into practice in their daily lives from moment to moment.

NEGATIVE EMOTIONS OR SYMPTOMS?

One of the most basic concepts that I wanted my patients to understand is that not every negative emotion is a symptom. Negative emotions are important for survival and comfort. They occur in reaction to a perception of threat in the environment and help to mobilize the body to handle the situation. The differences between warranted negative emotions and symptoms have to do with their basis in reality. Warranted negative emotions are in response to a real situation happening to you.

There are three basic negative emotions that occur in reaction to events in the environment: Fear, depression, and anger.

I. FEAR - There are three types of fear: fear itself, nervousness, and anxiety.

Fear is a state of alarm that is appropriate and warranted in response to physical danger. For example, if I had a lion in my office with you, you would feel fear. Prior learning would have you recognize the animal as a serious danger to your health and fear would be stimulated. Your body would be mobilized in a state of alarm either to fight off the lion as best you could or run for safety. If I removed the lion, your fear would reduce and your body would return to its prior condition.

But let me be a little more realistic. Let's say you're driving to the grocery store. You're taking the same route you always take because there's usually no traffic. You come to the stop sign at which you generally slow without stopping but this time, as you begin to enter the intersection, a car races by you with the right of way and blares his horn at your inattention. You slam on the brakes and you can feel your eyes as wide as dinner plates and your arm and leg muscles tight and bulging. You resume driving through the intersection as cautiously as a new driver who just received his license the same morning. Your pounding heart and the shakiness that you feel in your stomach and chest slowly recede.

The wide eyes, tight muscles, pounding heart, and shakiness are the body's reaction to fear. Clearly, you were in a situation of physical threat. Your body reacted by tensing for the blow and, with the danger past, eventually resumed normal functioning. Most importantly, you learned from the situation and will not take stop signs lightly in the future.

One more example: You're standing on a ladder changing a light bulb. You're short, so you're reaching. You reach a bit too far and you begin to slip. After some gymnastics, you maintain your balance and climb down, calming your increased heart rate, your throbbing head and quivering legs. You vow never to use the top step on a ladder again.

In the above situations, your body became mobilized against threat. It happened automatically and took some time to reduce after the threat passed. You learned from the experience and intend to change your behavior in the future.

Nervousness is mild fear that is produced in situations with no threat of serious physical harm but rather, a possible negative social consequence or disappointment from not attaining a goal you value.

An obvious situation that would generate nervousness is a first date with a person whom you really like and with whom you want to build a relationship. I'm sure you can remember an important first date in your past. You were on your best behavior, thought too much about what your date was thinking, and were the most considerate and wittiest person who ever existed, all to impress her into finding you attractive.

Remember the nervousness you felt during your first job interview? You dressed impeccably, even wore cologne or perfume. You worried afterwards that you hadn't said the right thing and that you appeared intelligent and a necessity to the company.

Another situation, more negative than the others, was your first traffic court appearance. You dressed in your best suit, tried to appear conservative, called the judge "Ma'am," admitted your stupidity and thanked her for the fine that you happily paid, signaling the conclusion of the agonizing ordeal.

Fear and nervousness share some similar characteristics. Both motivate and enhance performance. Intelligence solves the problem as to how to behave in order to relieve discomfort, either for your safety or to attain a goal.

With fear, the fight-flight mechanism is triggered and your intelligence will prompt you to fight for survival or retreat to safety. If the lion jumped at you, you would fight. In the examples of almost causing an auto accident and recovering your balance on the ladder, fear caused you to retreat for your safety.

With nervousness, intelligence directs behavior in order to attain your desired goal. You were on your best behavior during your first date, at the interview and in front of the judge.

Anxiety is a little different from fear and nervousness. Anxiety is fear that has no identifiable source in the environment. In other words, you must leave the present or current and travel to the future or into the thoughts of others to experience anxiety. Anxiety occurs in response to self-critical, out-of-control thoughts that you will fail to behave correctly while in a specific situation, and you can expect negative consequences to follow.

For instance, you're in a situation to meet some new people and your out-of-control thoughts scream at you, "I can't handle it. Everyone will know it and hate my guts, and laugh at me, or something else. I don't know what it will be, but I know it will be terrible." The thoughts are negative and the body responds with anxiety toward the unidentifiable threat, causing a spiraling, or escalation into an attitude of pending doom or catastrophe.

Anxiety is not a motivator that enhances your behavior as does fear and nervousness. The only motivation that comes from anxiety is to avoid and withdraw. The major problem with anxiety is that you don't know what you're fighting against. Unlike fear, which identifies your enemy in the environment as a lion, an accident or falling, or nervousness as on a first date, an employment opportunity, or before a judge, anxiety identifies the existence of some vague threat hiding to get you sometime in the future. The lack of structure of these thoughts allows anxiety to reach terribly high intensities.

Sandy was one of the most anxious people I had ever met. His anxiety effectively stopped him from doing as he liked. He anticipated hurting people and having them angry with him as a result. However, what was most noticeable concerning Sandy's anxiety was its ability to force him to avoid. He would actually cross the street to avoid the possibility of bumping into someone and offending them. This made for a difficult walk to work on a busy morning in northern New Jersey.

Jenny's anxiety kept her in her bedroom with "crazy" thoughts that she would hurt herself. Her thoughts generated anxiety over some negative future event and stopped her from doing as she wanted.

There's only one way to stop anxiety, don't leave the present. Attending to what is actually occurring in reality will reduce instances of anxiety. Remember, if you can't see, hear, smell, touch or taste it, don't think it. The chances are it will be negative, with symptoms to follow.

II. DEPRESSION - Depression can be reactive or clinical.

Reactive depression occurs in response to a loss that is observable in the environment. For instance, the death of a loved one generates depression that is usually severe. For those of us who have lost a loved one, I don't need to explain the unreality of the situation and the time it requires to return to some degree of normalcy. The grieving process may take years and is certainly uncomfortable.

Depression may also be a reaction to the end of a relationship. This loss is, in some ways, similar to the passing of a loved one but of course, not near the magnitude or severity. Missing the characteristics of the person as well as the activities spent together causes a longing and boredom that usually reduces as new activities and individuals replace the loss.

Other less severe reactive depressions may result from losing a favorite item such as a picture or a ring, moving away from friends and termination of employment. Here, depression is in reaction to the loss of cherished persons, activities, things, or situations. The loss is observable and real and, with time, you bounce back to focus on your surroundings as replacement of the loss begins to occur.

Clinical depression results from a style of avoidance that has you do what you don't want rather than what you want. For instance, you may say "yes" when you really want to say "no." You may avoid a situation in which you want to participate but feel too anxious. You may feel awkward in your behavior rather than spontaneous. You may miss a favorite TV program as a result of drifting. Even failure to adjust to a more comfortable position in your chair or not going for a walk when you want is avoidance of the expression of your taste. If you don't do as you like, you cannot engage your taste and cannot experience pleasure. Over time, as avoidance becomes a style in your behavior, depression sets in.

Although Fran's eating disorder and Sandy's anxiety and rituals appear quite different from one another, their symptoms were caused by the bad habit and each suffered depression. Both Sandy and Fran experienced the same sequence of the habit and, although other symptoms dominated, each was depressed. Depression occurs when you don't do as you like. As youngsters, Sandy felt guilt that something "bad" might happen at home if he stayed out with his friends and did as he liked and Fran did what she didn't want rather than face another lecture from her mother. Sandy and Fran developed some strange behaviors that certainly caught their attention and, in this way, prevented expression. However, each was depressed as a result of their avoidance. They saw their lives as a dead end. Each believed that they had never been happy in the past and felt hopeless that there could be a change for the better in the future.

The result of avoidance is monotony and boredom, or depression. Likable stimulation of the senses is necessary to experience pleasure. Avoiding situations in order to reduce anxiety from the habit will cause deprivation of pleasure since you are not experiencing events fully. The resulting depression leads to feeling trapped into living a miserable existence, with no hope of happiness and helpless to change the future. Depression, like anxiety, occurs in response to self-critical thoughts. Unlike anxiety thoughts that are specific, depression thoughts are big and wide and occur out of and away from specific situations where you must behave specifically. For instance, you're home and you think, "I never handle things, and I never will. I guess I'm stuck in this miserable life until I die." Expressing your taste will prevent clinical depression. Take a walk when you want. Move to a position that's comfortable. Walk loose. Get into life and live freely. Be yourself. If you are doing things that you like and enjoy, in other words, things that engage your taste, you will feel pleasure and your life will not be monotonous at all, but entertaining and exciting.

III. ANGER - Anger may take two forms: warranted and unwarranted.

Warranted anger occurs when you are treated maliciously by someone. At those times, ask for clarification and if maliciousness is undeniable, take action to protect yourself and retaliate if necessary. For instance, let's say you hear that a co-worker is speaking negatively about you. Rather than listening to the rumors and drawing conclusions, ask the co-worker for clarification. Should the co-worker deny the act, inform her that you have been hearing rumors without mentioning names and let the issue drop. Should the rumors stop, you have handled the situation. I like to ask for clarification at least twice so that I can be confident that my point was understood.

Should the rumors persist, and you're sure they may be traced to the same co-worker, make a complaint to management within the structure set by the company, detailing the series of steps which you have followed. In this case, your anger was warranted and you took intelligent steps to stop maliciousness. You sought to resolve the matter in an organized, logical manner.

Another form of warranted anger is frustration. Frustration occurs when your attempts to accomplish a goal are blocked in some way. For instance, let's say you own a classic car and want to put it in a show. The only problem is that you need a set of side mirrors. You order the mirrors from a company that promises delivery before the show but fails to make the deadline. You become frustrated and angry since the car was ready to show and now you can't enter it. Rather than walk around with anger that transforms into that familiar heat in your stomach, resign yourself to the fact that you will miss the show. Find another company with which to do business and go to the garage to wax the car so that it's ready for the next available show. In each case of warranted anger, intelligent decisions resulted in less discomfort.

Unwarranted anger comes from feeling trapped and controlled by your lack of expression. You tend to take differences of opinion personally, especially differences from others, which you interpret as criticism. As a result, you believe the world is against you and you're ready to be angry with people even before meeting them. You justify your misery by blaming everyone else for your failures when you haven't even tried to accomplish a thing and you feel perpetual anger toward your fabricated enemies.

Bill is the best example of unwarranted anger. He walked around with a chip on his shoulder, expecting criticism from people. His life revolved around his anticipation of criticism. He weight-lifted, used steroids, and was violent.

While Bill's anger was quite visible, anger in the other patients didn't seem so evident, but it was there. Each of them felt trapped and controlled by the habit and felt anger over their helplessness to change their situations. But unlike Bill, the others held their anger back for fear of offending and turned it inward onto themselves in the form of self-criticism. They used words like "stupid," "lazy" and "worthless" to describe themselves and expected nothing but a continuation of their misery in the future.

The problem with unwarranted anger, very simply, was that the patients were attending to out-of-control thoughts and not behaving according to their taste. Thoughts that your life is controlled by others and by unfortunate situations are nothing more than justification for your lack of effort or expression. Actually, the final decision in any situation is always yours. If you do what you don't want, you have given up control of your expression to out-of-control thinking. Even to give up control is your decision. It simply happens to be a bad one. You must remember that differences of opinion are not angry acts that offend, nor are differences from others criticism. They are simply points of view and everyone is entitled to have and express them, even you.

As you may see, warranted negative emotions are vital and necessary for the safeguard of our health and welfare. They should not be held back or dampened but, with proper expression, should lead to intelligent, problem-solving behaviors designed to eliminate the discomfort of conflict situations. The purpose of Attention Training is not to reduce warranted emotional expression but to eliminate the experience of anxiety, clinical depression, and unwarranted anger, since they are unnecessary and hurtful. Negative emotional expression requires an observable source in reality.

EMOTIONAL EXPRESSION CAN TRIGGER THE BAD HABIT

At times, appropriate negative emotional responses may trigger the bad habit to intensity and awareness. The reason is simple. The habit is built on the misinformation that expression is an angry act, which offends and warrants negative consequences. Since the expression of negative emotion is, in fact, the expression of taste, the habit will be triggered. The symptoms of the habit will be particularly intense in situations of conflict and negative emotional reaction because conflict indicates your expression will be met with an opposing view, and, as a result of the bad habit's influence, will certainly offend.

For example, let's say you're in line at a grocery store and a person attempts to push ahead of you. You inform the person there is a line and you refuse to allow him to get in front of you. Your response was appropriate but you begin to question yourself, thinking you may have been too harsh or maybe you should have said nothing at all. After all, what was the big deal? Now you begin to feel guilt that you may have offended someone, anxious that the person will be angry with you and that you may be out and a similar situation could occur again.

Try as best you can to avoid having the habit attach to situations of appropriate negative emotional responses. Slow your thinking and use your intelligence to see differences between warranted and unwarranted negative emotional expression. Understand your response was logical and warranted, given the circumstances. Should you have future or mind-reading thoughts, refuse to entertain them. Structure your thinking to the facts of the situation only and the habit thoughts will recede. You may have to work on the technique a bit, but the effort will be worth the result.

Although the tendency of the habit to attach to appropriate negative emotional responses surprised many of my patients, its latching on to positive emotional responses knocked them for a loop. Let me explain. You're at a friend's house and really having a wonderful time. You're <u>relaxed</u>, laughing, joking, telling stories, and enjoying yourself. But at home, after the get-together, you begin to question yourself. Did you go too far? Were some of the things you said off-color? Did you offend your friend? Now the anxiety begins, "I made a fool of myself (self-critical thought over a specific behavior) at my friend's house." (a specific place), followed by depression, "I never have a good time and I never will." (self-critical, big, wide thoughts).

The habit's tendency to attach to positive emotional responses is quite logical. The habit constantly constricts your spontaneous expression so that you will not offend. In this situation, you were relaxed and enjoying yourself. The influence of the habit was less at your friend's house and you were more spontaneous in your expression. At home, your thoughts, influenced more by the habit as a result of less activity and events to attract your attention, question that the "bad thing" occurred while you were less constricted and more expressive, thus generating anxiety. Your anxiety is followed by the habit thought that, although you enjoyed yourself, you shouldn't get used to it since your miserable life will soon resume, and depression is generated.

Whether an emotion is positive or negative is irrelevant since the habit possesses no intelligence and cannot see differences. It can't see, hear, smell, touch, or taste. Its only function is to eliminate the expression of your taste so the "bad thing" doesn't occur.

Jean wasn't a patient of mine; she was a secretary at the clinic where I worked in Jersey City. Jean would have anxiety attacks when she felt happy. It was as if she thought, "I don't know why I feel so good. Something must be wrong." The habit is triggered by any emotional expression, positive or negative. Negative, because you may offend. Positive, because you may let down your guard and allow the "bad thing" to escape and offend. You just can't win with the habit.

Slow your thinking. Remember that you are in a battle with the habit. Refuse to entertain out-of-control thoughts. If you were offensive, your friend would have told you. If it didn't come off his lips, he wasn't thinking it. Your enjoyment of the evening was your success against the habit. Be confident that you will win the war. Keep your focus in the present and get ready for a peaceful evening of sleep.

CHANGE CAN BE SCARY

I also found it important for my patients to understand that the bad habit is triggered by change, any change. I have seen patients who have had anxiety attacks in reaction to the change of seasons, ones who have had anxiety as a result of the change from day to night, and ones who had anxiety from changes in TV programming during the holidays.

Although my patients were totally confused by the connection between anxiety and the seemingly trivial changes in events, the connection was there. A reflex or habit has no intelligence. The bad habit is simply a neural pattern with the sole purpose of preventing expression so the "bad thing" doesn't happen.

Changes indicate that an out-of-routine behavior may be necessary. Spontaneous expression may occur and negative consequences may follow. As a result, anxiety is experienced, distracting you from the situation at hand and preventing expression. The content of the situation is irrelevant. What is relevant is that you may need to express your taste toward the change in the environment.

Sandy's compulsions and rituals functioned to create sameness as a defense against change that might require him to behave in a spontaneous, "different" manner that might contain the "bad thing." As a matter of fact, all the patients experienced anxiety in response to change. Symptoms distract attention so expression can't occur. Since the habit has no intelligence, any change, no matter how trivial, will trigger anxiety.

Slowing your thinking and allowing yourself to be deliberately focused so that you can use intelligence to see the situation for what it is will prevent anxiety or reduce it once the anxiety has been triggered.

SECOND THINKING

Whenever you get an impulse to do something, the habit will step in to prevent you from expression and enjoyment. For instance, suppose you're home cleaning and it's a beautiful day. You think that you'd like to go for a walk. Cleaning can be put off for an hour or so with no ill effect. You think, "I'd like to go for a walk." then, "Wait. Maybe I'd better not. There's a lot of people out there. Maybe I'll become uncomfortable, and I should be cleaning anyway." I call this type of out-of-control thought second thinking because of its placement after an impulse to express.

Second thinking works to have you question your taste with vague, negative thoughts. Vague thoughts cause greater discomfort since the enemy cannot be identified, leaving the imagination to spiral or climb into an attitude of pending doom or dread. Second thinking tends to be very effective in stopping spontaneity and helps to generate depression since you are not doing as you like and want.

For instance, Sarah questioned all her impulses. To her, they were wrong or bad. She buried herself in work, leaving her no time to enjoy herself. If she had an impulse to go for a walk or go out, she immediately found reasons to avoid the activity. It might be that she needed to work, had to clean the apartment, or simply that something might happen. Whatever the thought might be, it stopped her from doing what she wanted.

Be aware of second thinking and go with your first impulse. If the thought is negative and forces you to avoid, it comes from the influence of the habit. Be smart, do what you want and see that "bad things" don't happen at all. See that doing what you want allows you to enjoy yourself.

WAITING FOR THE OTHER SHOE TO FALL

Although patients respond well and quickly to the Four Points, many have the feeling that they are "waiting for the other shoe to fall." The feeling is common and comes from the bad habit. This negative thought is future thinking and attempts to make the patient believe he can never be happy and that, sooner or later, he will return to a life of anxiety, depression, anger and misery.

Many of my patients, once their symptoms reduced and they felt better, had thoughts that something "bad" was going to happen. The out-of-control thoughts lessened their awareness and triggered anxiety. In most cases, simply instructing them to pay no attention to the thought worked. However, Sam had a great deal of difficulty with the thought. His concern that something bad was going to happen when he felt good effectively triggered his anxiety and started his compulsions.

I asked Sam and my other patients to treat this negative thought like any other. Ignore the thought and focus out since they can only have the thought as a result of losing awareness of the environment. Consciously ignoring the thought tended to get rid of it and the accompanying symptoms rather quickly.

CRYING FOR NO APPARENT REASON

I have met some patients who complained that they cry spontaneously for no apparent reason. It seems to them that the crying comes out of nowhere and may occur at nearly any time.

Actually, there is a reason for every emotional response, even spontaneous crying. Instances of spontaneous crying come from the big, wide thoughts of depression. The thought is that "I have never been happy and I never will." The thought is not in words or pictures but is an attitude. This attitude leaves you feeling hopeless that there can ever be a change and, with defenselessness staring you in the face, you cry.

The scariest aspect of spontaneous crying is that it happens so quickly; you don't know where it came from. This lack of information sets off out-of-control thinking, which concludes in the extreme negative, suggesting you're crazy. If you spontaneously cry, know that it comes from the habit and focus out. You're doing something about your life; you're learning the new habit. Don't pay attention to habit thoughts, you can't win. Ignore them and redouble your efforts against the habit. Get angry at it.

OUTRUNNING THE PRESENT

One big problem for Sandy, as well as many of the other patients, was racing thoughts. I call this kind of thinking outrunning the present. Sandy's racing thoughts often had him confused as to where he was and what was going on around him. They triggered anxiety in him since they were negative and started his rituals and compulsions.

Outrunning the present is similar to the behavior of a hyperactive child. If you've ever seen or known one, it appears as if the child is attempting to move to a different geographic position before she is physically able to do so. It is as if the child reflexively needs to leave the present situation before she does something wrong or "bad." Outrunning the present is the adult counterpart to childhood hyperactivity.

Outrunning the present results from the habit's attempt to remove you from the present so that spontaneous expression is eliminated, preventing the "bad thing" from occurring. The "racing" quality of the thoughts gives you an indication of the urgency of the reflex to prevent you from awareness of the present, where expression may occur.

Outrunning the present thoughts pull you from the here and now. However, there are a few themes that appear different but have the same purpose since they intend to move to the future and away from the present. For instance, I have met a number of young adults and middle-aged people who have told me they wished they were in old age because living with anxiety and depression and the stress of expression is so painful. The thought of moving life along so the "bad thing" doesn't happen is outrunning the present. The thought that the "bad thing" may occur was so stressful these individuals preferred old age and death to the existence that they endured.

Another content common to outrunning the present in people who are unhappy with the life they are living centers around the justification that things will get better eventually, in the future. The problem is the future never seems to arrive. Instead of expressing tastes in the present and making the changes necessary to gain happiness, some individuals avoid expression in the present, wait for the future and, in this way, perpetuate their unhappiness. Waiting for change in the future is actually procrastination.

To deal with outrunning the present, I asked Sandy and all my patients to consciously and deliberately slow their thinking in order to limit racing thoughts and outrunning the present. If any had difficulty slowing their thoughts, they were asked to mentally relate the events taking place around them and their behavioral response to those events. For example, I can see that I'm walking toward my car, placing my hand on the door latch and pulling the door open. I turn sideways and slide behind the wheel and place my key in the ignition, turning the key forward. I hear the engine start, place the car in reverse, turn my head to see where the car is headed, and back out of the driveway. By relating my behavior consciously, I am deliberately slowing my thinking. The behavior of mentally relating events to yourself provides reality as a structure for your thinking, making awareness easier to maintain. Some practice in this technique will help you remain in the present and offset racing thoughts.

FEELING OVERWHELMED

A similar condition to outrunning the present occurs when an individual becomes overwhelmed with situations, events, or responsibilities. For example, say you have three important situations to take care of. None of the three is out of your ability to handle, but you have the habit. As you deal with the first, some of your attention is on the other two. With the first task completed, you turn to the second. Some of your attention anticipates the third task and some is now concerned you might have made mistakes with the first, since your attention was divided. When you're ready for the third, your mind is on the first and second tasks, since you know you weren't focused when you addressed them.

Once again, the solution to feeling overwhelmed relates to slowing your thinking. Consciously and deliberately focus on what's in front of you. Attend to the first task and consciously disregard the second and third. With the first completed, attend to the second. You don't need to be concerned with the first since you attended to it fully, and you will not allow distraction from the third since it is not yet before you. With the second achieved, you can now fully attend to the third.

Practicing this technique brings results quickly and supports the concept of the Four Points. For instance, let's say you are a housewife feeding your thirteen-month-old child while your six-year-old is asking you a question. Suddenly your phone rings and you hear the plumber knocking on the front door. You pull the spoon out of your child's mouth, causing the baby to cry, yell at your six-year-old who starts complaining that she didn't do anything wrong, pick up the phone and yell at your husband who called to ask how your day is going, slam the phone down, and run to the front door, with chaos erupting behind you.

The problem with the situation above is that you tried to handle items before you were able to. Your thinking was racing to the next situation before you took care of the one in front of you. As more stimulation or events occurred, you became overwhelmed and the result was anger with the irritants, your two children, your husband, and the plumber.

Let's say all these events happened at the same time. By consciously slowing your thinking, you would first only pay attention to taking the spoon out of your son's mouth and maybe giving him a pacifier, then turning to your daughter, you attentively ask her if she could please hold on a moment while you answer the phone and the door. You would then pick up the phone, say "hello" to your husband and ask him if he could call back in about ten or fifteen minutes since you need to answer the door. Finally, you walk to the front door, lead the plumber to the clogged drain, answer your daughter's question, and resume feeding your son.

The point of the matter is that you cannot do more than one thing at a time. If you give each your full attention, you will be able to accomplish more, with fewer symptoms and less anger directed toward those around you. Practice will develop the behavior into a habit so quickly you will be surprised with the success you achieve.

At times, you may feel overwhelmed when practicing the Four Points. With attention increased, you are actually closer to the current or present and therefore more able to express in response to what is occurring around you. The habit will be triggered at these times, and with increased stimulation to the senses, you may feel overwhelmed, as if too much is occurring at once. This condition could have you feel somewhat anxious, but, with practice, any anxiety you experience will lessen and finally decrease to zero.

You may mistakenly believe increasing attention or focus caused the anxiety. However, increased attention cannot cause anxiety. Actually, anxiety is generated by the bad habit in response to increased awareness. As you increase your attention thereby coming closer to the present where expression of taste may occur, the habit is triggered in an attempt to decrease your awareness and eliminate spontaneity. It is the habit pulling you inside your head, not the increase of attention and the resulting awareness, that generates the feeling of being overwhelmed and anxious.

Don't be concerned over this condition since continued practice will allow the body to become familiar with increased awareness so that discomfort cannot occur. Intelligently noticing the symptoms and understanding where they come from increases your awareness and decreases the influence of the bad habit, resulting in a reduction of symptoms.

MISTAKES ARE TEACHERS

A common problem for many patients is frustration when they make mistakes that lead to decreased awareness and symptoms. They somehow believe they should have recognized the situation before they were pulled in by the bad habit, and thus prevented the resulting symptoms. Self-criticism and anger only serve to reduce your energy and feed the bad habit. Believe me, the bad habit doesn't need any help from you; it does well on its own. You weren't born with knowledge as to how to develop the new habit. It must be learned, like riding a bike. Mistakes aren't evidence of inferiority or inadequacy; they are teachers. Every time you make a mistake, learn from it so it is less likely to occur in the future.

Sandy learned very well from his mistakes. He didn't take them personally but saw them as teachers. He tended to use the information from mistakes to increase his awareness and strengthen his new habit.

THE VALUE OF SITUATIONS

Confusion can occur as to why some situations continue to trigger the bad habit while others lose their ability to generate symptoms almost immediately. Intelligence enables us to see differences among situations, persons and events, and it places different value or importance on each. As a result, low valued items, since they are less important to us, lose their ability to trigger the bad habit much sooner than those of high value. Although high valued items decrease in their ability to trigger the bad habit as Attention Training progresses, their rate of decline is slower. The result is that high valued items will continue to trigger the bad habit until their influence or value reduces. Once lowered, a high valued item will drop like a rock and be unable to trigger symptoms. For instance, items pertaining to your spouse will be of higher value than items related to a stranger. You will be more prone to mind read your husband or wife than a guy in Asia whom you have never met. However, once you understand that differences of opinion are points of view, you will be able to express yourself to anyone in a tactful manner.

WORK AND FREE TIME

Some of my patients are at a loss to understand why they experience anxiety at home or during some activities like shopping or going for a walk, but not at work. Clearly, there is more pressure to perform at work than during free time. The reason is at work there is a protocol, a manner in which you must proceed in order to accomplish the task at hand. At work, you know how to behave. You don't have to guess or express your own opinion and taste.

Outside of work, in your free time when you are most purely yourself since you can do as you want, the habit is triggered and you will experience symptoms. Remember, the bad habit is there to stop you from expressing your taste. Free time is when you can watch TV, go for a walk, call a friend, or do nothing. The decision is yours. It is in this condition of pure expression when the habit will be triggered to stop your spontaneity. Be sure to be focused before you lose awareness. Once the habit is triggered, you lose intellectual control to the degree that you are pulled in with out-of-control thoughts and with anxiety to follow. Be slow in your thinking, and be aware of what is going on around you moment by moment.

However, some people do feel anxiety at work. Anxiety occurs when they feel they must express an opinion that reflects their taste in order to perform a task, and anticipate failure as a result. Again, slow your thinking, don't allow yourself to future think or mind read, stay focused and your anxiety will decrease.

CRISIS AND AFTERWARDS

Anxious and depressed people are often amazed at how well they handle crisis situations. Crisis situations occur in the present. You can observe them in your surroundings. As a result of a real situation, intelligence and the body are mobilized toward a condition of threat and can properly handle the emergency situation with accurate problem-solving behavior. Generally, the time when a person with the habit has difficulty with symptoms is not during the crisis, since intelligence is dominant, but after the crisis, when the habit is triggered with all kinds of thoughts that you probably did something wrong and there will be negative consequences. The thoughts and attitudes generate anxiety. Intelligent thoughts, using the Four Points, especially the fourth, ("If I can't see it, it doesn't exist. I'll handle it if it happens.") will reduce anxiety after a crisis.

LOUD THOUGHTS

Some of my patients have complained about thoughts that seemed as though two people were arguing inside their heads. This was the case with Billy. Sometimes Billy had thoughts that were clearly intelligent. They were logical, decisive and expressed his taste. However, habit thoughts would offer criticism and negative anticipation in an attempt to cancel out the intelligent ones, and therefore, prevent expression.

It wasn't that there were two voices inside Billy's head. Actually, he and you have one thought pattern that may, at times, be influenced more by intelligence than by the habit. Sometimes, the influence from each can occur so rapidly as to appear as if there are two distinct voices, with different personalities, speaking and even yelling inside your head, as was the case with Billy. Slowing your thinking, ignoring the thoughts, and using the Four Points to increase awareness help to eliminate this problem. The more awareness of the present, the less intense the symptoms of the habit.

Some patients may lose so much awareness toward the present that their negative thoughts actually flood their senses. At these times, not only do they hear their thoughts but actually see and feel them. This was the case with Billy's demons and the blood that he saw.

An interesting case that I'd like to mention is Carla. Carla was referred to me by my sister. The woman came from a religious background, which was quite critical of differences of opinion. As a result, Carla developed the habit at a very young age. By her teens, she was experiencing anxiety and depression and was hallucinating that she saw snakes, largely cobras, lots of them. At the time I first met her, Carla was fifty-three years old, had seen ten doctors and had been hospitalized on eight occasions for her condition.

When we started Attention Training, Carla was having anxiety attacks at work and home and was seeing snakes every day. By the third session, Carla's anxiety had reduced dramatically. She felt happier and was delighted with her expressiveness and how she felt. Her hallucinations had decreased to a couple times a week and only occurred during instances of stress and low energy. By session six, Carla explained that she felt as if she had been reborn and that the world had opened up to her. She was expressive, had no anxiety or depression problems, and was not seeing snakes.

Between sessions six and seven, Carla attended a weekend retreat. She came to her session and explained that while she meditated, although she didn't see snakes, she could feel them. I asked Carla to close her eyes and try to feel the snakes. She responded that she could. I then asked her to look in my eyes and try to feel the snakes. With increased focus, Carla told me that she couldn't. We resumed our session and I asked Carla to repeat the procedure of leaning out with me sporadically throughout the session. By the end of the session, Carla was able to close her eyes and, as hard as she tried, could not feel the snakes. The next session

Carla reported that if, in fact, she did see the snakes, she paid no attention and they were unable to upset her at all. Carla continues to do well. The snakes are no longer a problem for her. She no longer sees or feels them, and situations such as pictures of snakes on a PATH train advertisement are not able to upset her as they once had.

Carla has changed. Her boyfriend and co-workers have mentioned how delightful she is and Carla has found confidence that she never believed possible.

FEELING ANGRY WHEN YOU DON'T NEED TO

Many patients are confused by feeling anger when they become more expressive. Actually, the feeling of anger is common when patients progress. Attention Training requires a transition in your style from the bad habit to the new one. Since the bad habit cannot be replaced by the new one, its influence must be tapered down while the new one is strengthened. As anxiety reduces and you become more expressive, you may experience some anger as a result of years of feeling trapped and controlled. Some of your out-of-control thoughts will persist, but with a reduced intensity. The central thought, which stimulates anger, is that people will not accept your opinion and your expression will offend. Actually, the feeling of anger is a positive indication signaling that you are less anxious and more able to be expressive. However, your anger isn't necessary. You simply don't need to feel it. You can be expressive without feeling the discomfort of anger by realizing you are entitled to your opinion and that no one is capable of stopping you or changing your view. The thoughts that stimulate your anger are out-of-control and you should ignore them anyway. The final decision pertaining to your expression is always yours.

TENSION

As Attention Training progresses, you may notice you are able to be expressive without anxiety but you may experience uncomfortable tension. The new habit has developed to the point where tension has replaced anxiety. While tension is uncomfortable, it is a positive sign since it does not have the power to stop expression.

Anxiety is that "heady," unreal feeling that prevents expression. Your only thought is "I have to get out of here." Anxiety is a "stopper." Tension is muscular constriction that occurs when you believe you don't have the skill to behave appropriately in a situation. In other words, you don't believe you can express tactfully. Tension is handled in the same manner as anxiety. Slow your thinking; refuse the out-of-control thoughts and any other symptoms. Focus on reality in order to give yourself structure. If you can't see, hear, smell, touch, or taste it, it doesn't exist. You will handle it if it occurs, but you refuse to think and worry about anything negative.

ANXIETY, THE BAD HABIT AND THE GOOD ONE

Intense anxiety has a beginning, middle, and an end. The habit is constantly pressing attention inward, away from the events of the current. Some intelligence, influenced by the discomfort generated from the habit's press inward, attempts to justify the discomfort by attaching to an event that may be seen as threatening. Once attached, more attention is diverted from the present to further fabricate the nature of the threat and, as a result, anxiety intensifies. You may not be aware when the intensity first begins to mount. But, over time, usually a short time, discomfort gains intensity and comes to awareness. As the anxiety mounts, you do what you can to relieve the pain. You will act against it, and anxiety may recede below awareness and resume its usual low intensity press inward from the environment.

You didn't notice the decrease of attention until it was too late to intervene. Anxiety attacks occur when the decrease of attention is significant and rapid. Finally the anxiety decreases and you become more comfortable, but it is still there, beneath your awareness. Should you have your attention increased by consciously performing the Four Points before the habit attaches to an event, the chances are better that you will not suffer anxiety at all. Increased awareness will not allow the illogical fabrication.

Interestingly, after you have built the new habit to some degree, you will actually be aware of your attention loss as well as the habit's attempt to attach to an event. At first notice of decreased attention, you should turn away from the thought or symptom and focus toward the environment, preventing the intensification of symptoms and thereby reinforcing the new habit. With the new habit developed to some degree, usually after about three to five weeks of training, the notice of attention loss is automatic. Your attention is drawn to the loss of awareness, and your intelligence, realizing what is happening, refuses to engage the thoughts and symptoms. Consciously focusing toward your surroundings works to prevent more intense discomfort. You will actually notice your discomfort recede as intelligence increases.

Losing your attention and being pulled inside your head is disastrous. Not only do you experience the pain of symptoms, but your intelligence weakens. Your contact with the environment becomes foggy; you can't concentrate, remember, or think clearly. It seems any decision you make will be the wrong one. I suggest you make no important decisions when the bad habit has intensity since you will always make the wrong one. The reason is the habit will only prompt you to do what you don't want since it is based on the belief that behaving according to your taste will offend and warrant negative consequences.

Worst of all, in this state you tend to take everything personally. You believe anything you do or say will be misinterpreted by others and will offend them. The major characteristics of intelligence, the abilities to see differences among situations and to adjust your behavior to those differences reduces, and confusion increases.

Your intelligence, influenced by the habit and in an effort to identify the enemy, attaches to situations and events and has you take responsibility for anything negative that may or may not have occurred. For example, if someone is hurt or offended, you did it. Some individuals even feel responsible for a negative situation seen in a movie or on TV. I once had a patient who read a story in the newspaper and suffered anxiety that he might be responsible for a crime that had happened in Chicago, despite the fact that he lived in Jersey City. Of course, the answer to such situations is to prevent them from occurring by consciously focusing using the Four Points, before you get pulled in.

WHO AM I?

The bad habit has one purpose, the prevention of spontaneous expression. Because most individuals with the bad habit have learned it at a young age, I often hear those with it say, "How can I do as I want? I don't know what I like and don't like. I don't know who I am." And they don't. The habit has effectively stopped spontaneous expression in these individuals and they have lived their lives doing what they don't want rather than what they want. The result is many people with the habit have few interests. If we define the development of interests as occurring as a result of the expression of taste, then it is logical that these people would not have developed interests since the habit did not allow the expression of taste.

By focusing on the present, you will be able to determine what you like and what you don't like. With increased awareness, you will not be able to take differences personally so that expressing your taste will not cause anxiety. Over time, you will become familiar with your likes and dislikes and you will know who you are. You are your taste.

By now, I'm sure you've noticed the most important technique is to slow your thinking deliberately and consciously. With your thinking slowed, you may use any of the techniques mentioned.

However, with your thinking speedy and racy, you don't have a prayer.

Chapter VI

Thank You For Your Support

---

*"If the inward power that rules us be true to Nature,
it will always adjust itself readily to the possibilities
and opportunities offered by circumstances."*
Marcus Aurelius

Sandy couldn't believe it. I'd been seeing him for more than a year and we'd been through a lot together. Now it was beginning to turn our way. He felt some pride in that he had been with me through the development of RAD and Attention Training and often offered suggestions as to how to make improvements on the technique. But Sandy could be tough. He would question my ideas and in this way forced me to think harder about my directions and procedures, having me perfect them in order to accomplish the desired effect.

His compulsions, rituals, and anxiety had decreased to the point where Sandy was actually having some fun. He was able to comfortably engage in activities which he hadn't done since he was an adolescent. He could leave the house without apprehension, bump into someone, say, "excuse me" and think nothing of it. He could sit on a crowded bus without paranoid thoughts that people might think negatively of him and he could handle work. He even bought a new car at my urging. Although the car sat for a couple of weeks, he eventually began to move it back and forth in the driveway. Soon, he drove around the block and, despite inspecting the car for evidence of an accident, felt ecstatic to be driving the car at all. It wasn't long before Sandy was fairly symptom-free and engaging in most of the activities he had been forced to leave so many years ago. He wasn't done, we needed to make his new habit stronger, but it was happening.

Sandy was unusual because he experienced most of the symptoms my other patients endured. He had them all. It was for this reason I used Sandy's case to design the Four Points and to develop techniques to support contact with the environment.

Sandy and my other patients responded well to the procedures I had taught them earlier. Although performing the Four Points would eliminate problems in all areas, the special conditions, situations, and events the techniques focused on tended to reinforce the Four Points and helped them to understand the value of attention and awareness. It was as if the techniques translated the Four Points into a concrete format, which enabled Sandy and the others to see and understand awareness as a continuous process, no matter how minor or trivial a situation may appear.

I realized that patients didn't understand the habit and Attention Training as I did. I needed to be sensitive to how they understood the concept of increased awareness as a style of thought and behavior that was to become constant from moment to moment. I knew there were conditions and symptoms that Sandy and some of my other patients didn't equate with the bad habit.

As time went on, I found that converting more circumstances and conditions to the Four Points would help my patients improve their awareness in situations they had tended to take for granted. These situations were of very low value. They included events my patients thought little of but caused significant discomfort, and over time, developed into a style of thinking and behaving that locked them into the habit and a terrible life of symptoms.

Some of the techniques are so obvious they can be overlooked easily. I'm sure you have frequently used one or more of the procedures in the past and simply saw their positive results as logical. The difference with Attention Training is the techniques are organized in a systematic manner so you can most efficiently obtain the desired outcome, decreased symptoms and increased pleasure, as rapidly as possible.

NO LOOSE ENDS

A wonderful technique supporting contact with the present is to be consciously aware of handling situations as they occur and not to put things off or <u>procrastinate</u>. Situations such as mailing a letter, making a phone call, paying a bill, doing the laundry or any activity that requires attention has the effect of having you feel in control. Leaving <u>loose ends</u> has the opposite effect. Although you may not be able to remember the content of the tasks you put off, your mind and body will be left with the information that you didn't handle them. Your intelligence, influenced by the habit, will justify your avoidance with the thought, "I didn't handle them because I couldn't. If I had tried, I'd have failed." This negative thought eventually leads to an attitude of feeling out of control and will then trigger anxiety, more avoidance, and a perpetuation of the sequence of the bad habit.

Handling situations as they occur not only pertains to physical tasks such as making a phone call, but also to expressing your taste. For example, let's say some of your friends tend to ignore or disregard your opinion. They may call at the last minute to invite you to attend an event, ask you for a favor they know may be inconvenient for you, volunteer you for functions without your knowledge and so forth. Because you have the habit, you hold back expression but, in addition, because the situations involve a difference of opinion, you reflexively foresee conflict and anger, and you become anxious, anticipate what is expected and comply. You justify your avoidance by telling yourself, "No big deal. Why make a fuss over such a trivial thing?" So, you let it go. You consciously forget about these situations, but they actually stay on your mind, not in terms of what they were, but instead, how you handled them. Your avoidance of expression converts into an "out-of-control" attitude that generates anger and accumulates over time so that during one of these "trivial" situations, you blow up, out of proportion to the event. Your friend, who may not know that you were offended at all, is stunned by your behavior and you feel foolish and guilty, reinforcing the idea you should not express yourself because of your tendency to hurt others.

However, loose ends may also involve the expression of your taste in what you might consider minor situations and events. Not going for a walk when you want, avoiding an activity in which you would like to participate, even not changing your position to be more comfortable is leaving loose ends.

Situations like these are not as trivial as they may appear. Your mind remembers you didn't handle the situation regardless of its value, setting up an out-of-control attitude and anxiety. It's easiest to express when these situations first occur since they don't have high value and can be handled without complication. By expressing as situations occur, you're able to prevent a recurrence of similar situations and reinforce expression as well as an attitude of being in control.

The goal is to have a clear mind. Taking care of what is in front of you is important to maintain contact with the present and to feel in control. Whether it be a situation or an event, trivial or important, dealing with the issue at hand requires expression and allows you to move on without unfinished business on your mind.

THE INABILITY TO SAY "NO"

A condition that is quite common to the habit is the inability to say "no." Individuals with the habit don't want to make waves. They believe if they don't comply with another's request they will offend and receive anger in return. As a result, they do what they don't want, a situation that generates anxiety over social interaction and depression, since they avoid expressing their taste and doing what they like.

Sandy's overload at work is an example of his inability to say "no." He and many of my other patients would actually avoid some social situations because they anticipated having to comply with someone else's request.

The inability to say "no" comes from the bottom line of the habit, the tendency to take differences of opinion personally as angry acts that offend. Stop and think about it. An opinion or a decision is not an angry act; it is a point of view. You and everyone else are entitled to your perception of the world and to your taste. Angry acts are intentional and malicious attempts to hurt others. If your decision is an expression of your taste and not malicious, it doesn't qualify as an angry act and you should not feel guilt or think you will offend.

I know saying "no" will be difficult in the beginning. Try consciously to say "no" in low valued situations first. Once you've mastered these situations, move up to higher valued ones. If you do as you don't want, you will become depressed over time.

One more thing: Be aware of people who try to have you feel guilt if you don't do as they want. These people are trying to manipulate you. Don't become angry, no one can make you say "yes" if you want to say "no."

LEAVE SITUATIONS KNOWING WHAT TOOK PLACE

One excellent technique related to handling what is in front of you is to leave situations consciously aware of your thoughts and actions and the events that have occurred. This exercise contributes to the feeling of being in control and supports the Four Points. The technique has you structure your thoughts with reality and, in this way, helps to keep you anchored in the present while reducing the potential of out-of-control thinking. Leaving a situation knowing what took place is a bit more specific than not leaving loose ends. The procedure not only helps to build an attitude of feeling <u>in control</u> but also helps to reduce sleep problems as will be discussed in a later section.

LOADING UP WITH INTELLIGENCE

There were some specific situations on which Sandy placed high value. As a result, the habit would attach to them having Sandy take the event too seriously and triggering symptoms. I asked him to identify these situations and to "<u>load up</u>" with intelligence before entering them. For instance, before Sandy entered work, he stood outside the building for a moment and allowed the air, wind, sky, and sound to flood his senses. Once he increased his attention, he entered the office and tried to maintain his level of awareness for as long as he could. After some practice, Sandy was able to place the situation in proper perspective and his anxiety at work began to decrease.

Knowing the situations on which you place high value gives you an advantage over the habit and its symptoms. You know the bad habit will hit you with thoughts and symptoms in certain situations. However, if you increase your attention and awareness prior to entering the situation, you will have a greater degree of intelligence and a greater resistance against the bad habit. With stronger intelligence and logic working for you, the hit from the habit cannot be as intense as it would be if you had not "loaded up."

LEANING OUT WITH INTELLIGENCE

In situations where you are already experiencing mild anxiety, you may "lean out" with intelligence. Simply increase your focus using any or all of the Four Points. The increased intelligence will act to blow away any anxiety and you may resume your activity with comfort. Leaning out works for situations in which you are only mildly anxious.

CHANGING THE SCENE

Another technique similar to leaning out and loading up with intelligence is changing the scene. In situations where you have noticed anxiety at a low level you may change the scene by looking away from the events to which the habit has attached in order to experience different stimulation. For instance, you're walking on the boardwalk in Belmar, you see people approaching from the opposite direction, and you become anxious from mind reading thoughts. Change the scene. Look at the clouds in the sky or the waves hitting the shore. Or let's say you're at a club speaking to some people and you feel anxiety. Change the scene by talking to your friends about the band, then by watching the guitarist's fingers moving along the strings or the drummer's sticks moving in the air and coming down on the skins of the drums.

Changing the scene allows different stimulation to reach your senses. The effect is to increase your attention and awareness. As a result, your anxiety will decrease and you may resume your walk, conversation or whatever you were doing with increased focus and less habit thinking.

STIMULATE YOUR SENSES

At times Sandy found himself becoming anxious after he had already entered a situation. For these occasions I asked Sandy to excuse himself, go outside and lean out with intelligence or go to the washroom and splash some cold water on his face. He was to stimulate his senses in order to increase his focus and therefore, his awareness. With his senses stimulated and his intelligence increased, Sandy could return to the situation with his thoughts slower and his symptoms reduced.

Like Sandy, you can use this technique when you feel anxious in a situation. Stimulating your senses will tend to increase your attention and awareness and reduce your anxiety.

LEAVING A SITUATION

There will probably be times when you may lose too much attention, therefore making recovery very difficult. At these times, try to remove yourself from the situation any way that you can. I once had a patient who had just entered Attention Training. He was motivated, happy to have an answer for his symptoms that made sense, and worked hard to develop the new habit. He came to an appointment proud as a peacock, and told me he had an anxiety attack at a grocery store, but stuck it out. He related how difficult it was and how he had to rest for the remainder of the day, but he fought back. After admiring his courage and resolve, I told him I

117

would rather he leave a situation where the habit gained too much strength. He became confused and I explained he'd been blindsided. He wasn't aware of the habit until he was deep inside his head and experiencing intense symptoms. I explained to him the habit is constantly attempting to eliminate expression by having him divert attention from the environment. Although the pressure from the habit may initially be low in intensity, he was constantly constricted whether he could feel it or not. At times, the intensity of the habit and the resulting symptoms may increase quite rapidly. Remaining in the situation may only serve to feed the bad habit and increase symptoms.

When you're in a situation to express and therefore closer to the present, the habit will gain in intensity, reducing your awareness. You will probably not realize the intensity of the habit until you feel symptoms. At times, the intensity of the habit may increase quite rapidly, catching you off guard and leaving you with no way out. This is the case in an anxiety or panic attack. If you feel you've been blindsided and the intensity of your symptoms is too strong to overcome, try to be social and offer a logical excuse, but leave the situation. Realize that the habit is strong, and you don't want to play to its power. Leave the situation until your new habit is stronger. Wait until the cards are in your favor. Be smart.

Choosing to leave a situation is an intelligent decision, not avoidance. Decisions come from intelligence. A decision is a choice, reflecting your taste. Avoidance, caused by the habit, doesn't offer a choice. With avoidance, you are forced to do what you don't want.

GOOD AND BAD DECISIONS

A simple rule to remember is that good decisions are intelligent thoughts and cause you to feel good, while bad decisions are habit thoughts and cause you to feel bad. Intelligent thoughts and decisions are always positive and reflect your taste. As a result, they will make you feel good. Bad decisions are habit thoughts that have you avoid the expression of your taste and do what you don't want. As a result, you will feel bad.

SLEEP DISTURBANCE

There are special problems related to the habit that we need to address. One is <u>sleep pattern disturbance</u>. Sandy complained of sleep problems. Some nights he couldn't sleep at all, but mostly, Sandy's sleep was, at best, broken. One thing was for certain, no matter how Sandy slept, he would always wake up in the morning exhausted and in his head, with decreased attention directed toward the environment.

The reason for Sandy's sleep pattern disturbance was the habit. Sandy's awareness was decreased throughout the day. This decreased awareness resulted in reduced information coming to the senses. He would leave any situation feeling out-of-control, not really sure what had taken place. This condition left his body in a chronic state of alarm. His activity during the day was able somewhat to distract him from his terrible thoughts. However, at night, without the distraction of the day's activities and in his attempt to sleep, the habit would surface, sometimes in words or pictures, but mostly in an attitude. The negative thoughts triggered an intense state of alarm in Sandy's body that was incompatible with the relaxation necessary for sleep, and Sandy would suffer insomnia. Sandy passed many sleepless nights pacing and anticipating tomorrow's trials and recounting the day's events, reviewing what he might have done to offend someone.

On nights when he was exhausted from his worry and sleeplessness, Sandy would finally sleep, but the state of alarm continued and his sleep was light and fitful with anxiety attacks waking him, all resulting from his negative thoughts. If he dreamed he would have nightmares. <u>Nightmares</u> are nothing more than out-of-control thoughts that occur while a person sleeps. During the day, Sandy's out-of-control thoughts had some basis in reality even though they were illogical. For example, despite the impossibility of Sandy's thought that he had touched a woman boarding a bus across and up the street, there actually was a woman boarding a bus. Although he never hit another car or a pedestrian, Sandy did drive. However, while asleep, without the benefit of any intelligent contact with his surroundings, Sandy's thoughts were totally influenced by the habit and his state of alarm. His dreams could take any form. They could involve dead people running after him, falling eternally up or any other bizarre content. However, the content of the dreams was not important. What was most telling was the theme of the dreams; they were always negative and out-of-control.

To remedy his sleep problem and in support of the Four Points, I asked Sandy to try to be more attentive throughout the day and to realize his increased awareness. I wanted him to use the technique of leaving situations consciously aware of what had taken place. The idea was to develop an in-control state of mind for Sandy. Sandy was faithful to the technique. He would consciously consider what took place after leaving a situation, certain to be concrete and not to allow assumptions. Sandy would use the technique whether he left a situation at work, with relatives, on the bus or even in front of the TV. After about ten days of leaving situations knowing what took place and increasing his awareness in a general way, Sandy's sleep improved dramatically.

There are times when you may dream vividly concerning events that are actually occurring in your life. These dreams have a basis in reality and reflect the value you place on the event. Such dreams as these are common given the importance you place on the event. They may be positive or negative, but they do have a concrete connection with reality and are not a symptom of the bad habit.

In vivid dreams, the events are actually taking place in reality. Their value is high and appropriate. Some events may include the death of a loved one, a new relationship, or a promotion to a new position of employment. Out-of-control thoughts during bad dreams are just that, out-of-control thoughts. They are negative, extreme and have little basis in reality.

ACHES AND PAINS

Another troublesome symptom of the habit is muscle ache. Muscle ache is caused by tension. Tension is muscular constriction resulting from holdback of expression.

Since the bad habit attempts to eliminate spontaneous expression, motor movement becomes constricted so your style, reflecting your taste, cannot be conveyed. Individuals with the habit often suffer chronic tension. Although usually not noticed consciously, the tension is experienced as ache in different areas of the body. Most common is ache behind the neck and between the shoulders. Sometimes the ache may be felt in the arms and/or the legs. At times, the chronic ache may be replaced by a numbness resulting from muscle fatigue. Tension headache is another common result of constriction from the habit and stomach disorder may also result from tension.

I ask patients to be aware of physical constriction and tension. I want them to consciously relax their muscles, to make them soft. In addition, I ask them to try to behave freely and fully. For example, when you walk, let loose, get into it. Walk, talk, sit, wave your arms, laugh, and behave as freely and as fully as possible.

The development of the new habit was quite evident in Sandy and the others. They became more animated. They actually looked better as a result of the reduction of constriction and tension in their bodies.

WILL I BE A MONSTER?

Many of my patients expressed concern over the outcome of Attention Training. They were concerned they might turn into ruthless monsters without feeling and compassion for others. Many believed "If I do as I want, I will be selfish and uncaring." Referring to your expression as coming from a "ruthless monster" or to yourself as "selfish" is evidence of the habit's influence to have you believe differences of opinion to be angry acts that offend. If you do as you like, you are self-centered and "selfishly" disregarding the opinions of others. The habit causes you to believe that if you express, you will be insulting people in a rude and callous manner, leaving them hurt, offended, and angry with you. This misconception acts to stop expression cold and effectively prevents the development of the new habit.

These statements are evidence of the habit as a tendency to view expression of taste as an angry act that will offend. Differences of opinion are points of view, not angry acts. All of us are entitled to have an opinion and to express our taste.

Most anxious people are actually quite tactful and socially aware in their expression, they simply don't express. From the influence of the habit, you will think you must agree with the opinions and tastes of others or face negative consequences. Anxiety stems from the habit thought that expression will offend. As a result, anxious individuals are oversocialized and worried about breaking rules that simply don't exist. They are generally very skilled socially and their expression would be conveyed with tact and regard for the feelings of others if not held back by anxiety.

Different from anxious people and inconsiderate for the feelings of others are individuals who have learned to care for themselves to the exclusion of those around them. These people are the con artists or the something-for-nothing takers. They lack consideration and empathy for others, don't ordinarily suffer anxiety, and have no wish to change their behaviors. It is unlikely that these individuals would read this book.

Some individuals feel guilt for expressing a difference of opinion to others. <u>Guilt</u> is a nasty feeling that should result from the conscious and malicious intent to hurt someone. However, guilt is inappropriate in response to expressing an opinion or making a decision. Guilt, in response to an opinion of taste, is evidence of the habit's ability to have you take expression as an angry act. Should they feel guilt, I ask my patients to question whether they expressed an opinion or intended to offend. The answer that the expression was an opinion or decision relieves the guilt. The procedure may need to be repeated for a time but soon the guilt will disappear and you will come to see expression of taste as appropriate social interaction, rather than an angry act intended to offend and hurt.

The tendency to view differences as angry acts is the reason some people often perceive expressiveness as aggression, and therefore, feel intimidated. Actually, expressive people are a delight. They tend to be happy and considerate and focused on the current. They are warm and nonassuming, as well as intelligent and accepting. The habit may cause some to view expressiveness in others as the "bad thing" occurring in the other person. The reaction of the habit's influence will be for the individual to justify, identify and fabricate the idea, that should they themselves be expressive, distaste, anger and social isolation will occur.

KEEP MOTIVATION HIGH

As you can see, much information is necessary to have a patient feel better. I try to convey this information to a new patient as soon as possible. The education begins during the first session. I begin by explaining the sequence of the bad habit and the Four Points. My objective is to have the patient leave with the tools to develop the new habit and an explanation for her symptoms. However, after a few sessions of hard work and progress, some patients seem to lull into a lesser state of motivation. They work less and don't deliberately use the Four Points to build the new habit, but rather, use them only to get out of trouble. I emphasize to them the importance of maintaining a high level of motivation in order to develop the new habit as quickly as possible. The lull that some of my patients experience is the result of resistance from the bad habit to devalue, or make light of awareness and the Four Points, and to forget to be focused. Explaining the condition helps to offset symptoms which occur when she forgets to be consciously focused so that the body goes back to what it knows best, the bad habit.

RECHARGING YOUR BATTERY

Recharging your battery is not so much a technique as it is a good idea. We live in a hectic world. Most of us are constantly on the go, being responsible, and taking care of business. Often our energy supply decreases, not so much as a result of the bad habit, but because we eventually get tired. Of course, decreased energy can upset your day and could trigger the bad habit. Recharging your battery simply refers to taking a break from activities such as work or another function, which requires sustained attention and effort.

Psychological energy is restored by stimulation to the senses. If you think about it, I'm sure you can recall a time when you felt energized by enjoying a situation. For instance, you felt energized arriving at the beach and seeing the ocean on a hot summer day, or looking to the sky at night and seeing a shooting star. Remember how you felt? It was an exhilaration. Or let's say you're driving to a destination and you're in the car for a while. You feel stiff and fatigued. Just stopping at a rest area and stretching increases your energy and you're able to drive on feeling fresher than before.

Of course, if you're at work or some other activity that requires your participation, you may not be able to take a stroll in the park. However, you may be able to take five minutes to go outside and look at the clouds and feel the breeze. At the office I simply look out the window for a few seconds and feel energized. It really doesn't take much. Just recharge frequently. A few seconds here, a few seconds there, will make quite a difference in how your day progresses.

THE ROLE OF MEDICATION

Some patients come to me from doctors and treatments that include the use of medication. Some of them believe that since I'm a psychologist and perform an intervention that recognizes a reflex to cause symptoms, I oppose the use of medication. Actually, I believe medication to be a worthwhile tool to fight symptoms. Although I believe it to be overused, the intelligent application of medication may well reduce troublesome symptoms that hinder a patient's work in Attention Training. Actually, I have advised medication for some of my patients. I always refer them to Jim, my psychiatrist friend, who prescribes appropriately without overmedicating, and with the intention of reducing dosage to zero when it is no longer needed.

For those patients who arrive at my office already using medication, I recommend they continue with their psychiatrist and I leave it to the patient and that doctor to determine when dosages should be reduced and then terminated. The use of medication, when employed properly, helps individuals with intense symptoms to benefit from Attention Training faster since it decreases interference from the symptoms of the bad habit.

HOW TO EVALUATE YOUR PROGRESS WITH ATTENTION TRAINING

It is easiest to assess your response to Attention Training on a weekly basis. You should look for decreases in the frequency, duration, and intensity of the symptoms that you experience. If you find that discomfort has decreased, then you're moving in the right direction.

Although the first week will be the hardest, you will notice, as a result of understanding where your symptoms come from and practicing the Four Points, that the frequency or number of instances when you feel uncomfortable will decrease. The duration, or length of time that your symptoms are experienced will lessen and the intensity, or the severity of your symptoms, will reduce. The decreases will continue as you practice the Four Points until the new habit is fully developed. By that time, not only will your symptoms and discomfort decrease to near zero, but you will notice increases in the frequency, duration, and intensity of pleasure.

This is when you begin to have fun. It's like being reborn and discovering a whole new world that has opened up to you. As the new habit becomes stronger, it will literally become "stupid" to think out-of-control. The key is repetition. Perform the Four Points until they become reflexive, second nature. Remember, practice, practice, practice.

All the techniques and conditions mentioned above are in support of the Four Points. If you're performing the Four Points consciously and intentionally you will be executing these techniques as well. However, the resistance from the habit will have you forget to be focused or believe that focus in some situations is unnecessary. At such times, the bad habit will remind you that you're not focused by generating symptoms.

Forgetting to be focused will occur. No one can remember to be consciously aware twenty-four hours a day. When you do forget and experience symptoms, don't be alarmed or upset. Simply begin the Four Points once again. Sooner, rather than later.

The Four Points are designed to build the new habit, not to get you out of trouble. If you are consciously performing the Four Points, you will prevent reduced awareness and symptoms. For most people whom I see, a period of three to five weeks is necessary to develop the new habit and longer to strengthen it. You will know you have the new habit because it will become easier to focus. As a matter of fact, your attention will stabilize at a higher level. Your symptoms will reduce in intensity, and your intelligence will be stronger. You will be less prone to take differences personally and events that would, in the past, upset you and trigger the habit will lose at least some of their ability to generate symptoms. Events on which you have placed high value will take longer to lose their potential to trigger symptoms, but they too will eventually be placed in a proper perspective and will decrease in intensity.

After some repetition of the Four Points, you will work less to increase your focus, since your attention toward the environment will, to a point, be automatic. You will feel more comfortable, have more energy, and be more efficient in all you do.

What you have developed is not a behavior so much as a style of thinking, perceiving and behaving. Although the new habit is young, it is very powerful and will automatically help you maintain contact with the current. You will notice your attention will automatically be drawn to any decrease of awareness, and your intelligence will consciously direct your focus outward toward the world. You will be aware of the bad habit, but it will not have the strength to hurt you so long as you maintain your focus. Higher valued items will continue to give you some trouble, but if you keep your thinking slow and deliberate, these items will not trigger the bad habit to any significant or high intensity.

The problem of the habit is not in your mind, but in your body. To prove this fact, think of a time when you were very focused on your surroundings. For instance, you were at a party or at a baseball game or any other event where your attention was increased and you were enjoying yourself. At those times your thinking was decisive. You could concentrate and remember. You couldn't take differences of opinion personally, and you were symptom-free. Now take a time when you lost your focus and you were <u>inside your head</u>. Then, your thinking was terrible. You couldn't concentrate, remember, or make decisions. You took differences of opinion personally and you experienced all kinds of symptoms, especially anxiety and holdback.

This fact indicates that the symptoms you experienced were not in your mind at all but in your body as a reflex. Literally, the quality of your thinking and how you feel, indeed, the quality of your life, depends on the degree of your awareness of the environment.

Attention Training is a technique that works on the physical cause of symptoms. Your intelligence is always potentially stronger than the bad habit. You can do anything you want if you're focused. If you remember to stay focused toward the environment, your symptoms will decrease and the physical principles which govern the body ensure the new habit will be developed.

However, if the new habit is to be developed efficiently and accurately, three characteristics are necessary for anyone attempting Attention Training. First, you must really want to make a change from the misery of the habit to a better way of living. Second, you must hold your goal to change in the highest regard. You must make change the most important goal in your life because without change, you don't have a life. Last, you must do the work. Although Attention Training may be hard at times, it is not as hard as living through your symptoms. You must be determined to do what is necessary to obtain the change you desire.

Although you have the new habit, you are not finished. You may notice that your symptoms have decreased and you tend not to take differences as personally as you did previously. But the new habit must be made so strong that the bad one cannot be triggered to intensity. Now, you must repeat the Four Points until they become second nature, until it becomes stupid for you to worry and until thinking and behaving with focus is the only way to be. Then you can find pleasure in the environment and be happy.

I define pleasure as a condition of likable stimulation to the senses. Happiness is the condition in which you habitually place yourself in likable situations. With the new habit strong, you will only be able to do as you like. You will not be able to do what you don't want. The only exception is when you do as you don't want out of consideration for another. In this situation, doing what you don't want becomes a "want" because you behave for the pleasure and benefit of an individual whom you value.

The new habit, when strong, sets up a condition that has the body seek pleasure. This is a physical condition and outside your conscious control, rendering the bad habit powerless to pull your attention from your surroundings and put you inside your head.

Until the new habit is firmly established, all you have to be concerned with is relapse.

Chapter VII

Relapse

---

*"To the nature of the vital force animating our bodies,
any frustration of the senses is an evil, and so is
the frustration of any endeavor."*
Marcus Aurelius

A <u>relapse</u> is a temporary period when you forget to be consciously aware and your body actually returns to what it knows best, the bad habit. It will feel as if you never learned the Four Points and never had the new habit. You will be dazed and confused, with out-of-control thoughts hitting you from everywhere and from nowhere at the same time. Anything you think will be negative. Your intelligence will be weak and nearly useless. You will know you're in a relapse but you will be almost helpless to get out of it. Your most troublesome symptoms will return with a vengeance, or at least you will think so, largely because you have not experienced them in such a long time. Relapses are no fun, but let's see what's going on.

Attention Training does not replace the bad habit; rather it develops a different habit, separate and distinct from the bad one. It's designed to train the body to respond to the environment in an opposite manner from the bad habit. Literally, through the intelligence, awareness is taught to the body. Once developed, the new habit competes with the bad one and dominates because it is based on pleasure, while the bad habit causes pain. The body actually chooses the new habit because of the Pleasure Principle. Should the body for some reason not have the new habit available to maintain contact with the present, it will have to resort to another method for contact. Unfortunately, the bad habit is the only other style that remains in the body and that is used for contact at the time of relapse. Any decrease in the strength of the new habit will result in the bad one filling the void left by the decrease, since contact with the environment must be maintained by the body. Although the body eventually forgets the behaviors of the bad habit, the weakening of the habit to disintegration takes some time. Until atrophied, the bad habit is used during a relapse because, honestly, I don't know how to dismantle it. I had tried to argue it out of existence with Sandy and was not happy with the meager results as well as the time and effort required. All Sandy and I were doing was counterpunching. The habit would hit Sandy and we would punch back with intelligence. This technique was not at all efficient. As hard as I tried, I could not put Sandy in front of the habit to stop it. It was too fast. As soon as it hit him, it was everywhere. He couldn't control it.

The bad habit is much older than the new one. As a result, its path to the brain is very well established and efficient. If attention toward the environment decreases for some reason, the bad habit automatically and instantly fills the void left by the portion of the new habit that has receded. How intense your symptoms are will depend on how much of the new habit has receded and how much of the bad one has filled the void. Once the bad habit has occupied the void left by decreased attention, it resists replacement by awareness by distracting you with out-of-control thoughts and other symptoms. It attempts to gain additional control by distracting attention with more intense symptoms.

The new habit is pleasurable which makes it very powerful and, when fully developed, causes the body to seek it. This is why your attention is automatically drawn to notice any decrease of awareness to rid you of discomfort and to restore pleasure. Just as your attention is drawn to a pinprick or a burn from a hot iron so that your intelligence reflexively removes you from the source of discomfort (you jump away), the same is true of the new habit. As the new habit strengthens, you'll notice your attention is drawn to decreased awareness and your intelligence will focus you out, away from out-of-control thoughts, refusing to go where you will be hurt.

Once the new habit is developed fully, it will not allow decreased attention and relapse. Over time, the bad habit will disintegrate with disuse, just as you may forget the route to a destination you once frequented because you no longer go there. In the same way, since the new habit doesn't allow the bad one to be triggered, the body will forget the sequence of the bad habit and symptoms will not be experienced.

I don't know how long it will take for the bad habit to disintegrate. It is logical that it will be present in the body for some time and at full capacity. However, until your awareness is completely automatic, you can have the new habit dominate the bad one by keeping the Four Points and increased awareness on your mind.

The condition of relapse can be of low or high intensity. It may last for less than a second or can endure for days. Sandy experienced some of the longest and most intense relapses I ever witnessed. A relapse for Sandy might last for more than two months. But why do relapses occur?

The body runs on <u>energy</u>. We eat, sleep, exercise and try to keep ourselves fit and out of harm's way. These activities provide us with energy, which allow us to grow from childhood and maintain health throughout life. However, should energy reduce for some reason, we find that our bodies are not able to function to capacity. The body begins to take care of basic needs and leaves higher functions, such as play and exercise, as too expensive for the remaining energy supply. The same is true for the new habit. Despite the fact that the new habit is pleasurable, it is quite young and less established in the body as compared to the bad one. In times of energy depletion, the body, for economy, will return to the bad habit. This is a relapse.

PRESSURE

I refer to any event, situation, or condition that reduces your energy and, therefore, leaves you vulnerable to relapse, as a pressure. Pressure can be categorized into three groups, explained below.

1. _Illness and Medical_. If you have a cold or some other illness, your energy will reduce as a result of your body's attempt to fight off the disease or hurt. When energy reduces, you will be prone to relapse. Your body will go back to the bad habit, since maintaining the new one expends too much energy. At these times you will be hit with out-of-control thoughts. They will not attach to situations with any degree of intensity unless you pay attention to them. Should you give them attention you will be drawn in more deeply and could experience symptoms. One major symptom you will experience, and is common to illness, is irritability. Your fuse will be shorter since you don't have the energy to be patient with situations, events, and people whom you ordinarily handle with ease. When you're ill, slow down. Be more deliberate in your focus. Recognize you don't feel well and blame the illness for your habit thinking, irritability, and any other symptoms that you may experience. Don't get frustrated; it's a condition that will end when you feel better. If you can put things off until you feel well, consciously decide to do so. Get rest. If you can't rest and must handle some situations, do them slowly and deliberately. Take it easy. Put things in perspective. Most anything can wait until you get to it.

Menstruation, menopause, and pregnancy are not illnesses, they are medical conditions, but they will reduce your energy level as well. Under these conditions, do as above. Slow down, recognize that your energy is reduced as a result of the condition and put off what you can. If you can't put things off, do what you must slowly, and try to rest. Expect to have out-of-control thoughts and you will be irritable but remember, your out-of-control thoughts won't attach unless you pay attention to them.

2. *Fatigue*. If you work too much, lose sleep, or fail to rest in order to restore your energy level, you will become tired. You will experience out-of-control thoughts and irritability. Do as mentioned above. Try to get rest. Blame the fatigue for any symptoms and slow down.

3. *High Value*. High value is the most common pressure that leads to relapse. If you place too high a value on an event, you will regard it as serious, and the habit will be triggered with intensity. This is how out-of-control thoughts work to generate symptoms. The thoughts are generated to justify the discomfort of decreased awareness and to relieve confusion. As a result, the thoughts must have some value, importance, or worth. A thought concerning a thing that you don't care about would not be of sufficient value to justify your discomfort and reduce your confusion. The content of the thought must be important to you. The thoughts must be out of the present since there is no real source for your discomfort in the current. If there was, your discomfort would be a real reaction to a real situation. Your intelligence would automatically problem-solve a response to handle the situation and reduce your discomfort. Without the structure of reality, the thoughts become way out of proportion and unreal, finally spiraling into an unidentifiable negative attitude. Let's look at the bad habit a bit differently. The problem is that some portion of your thoughts influenced by the habit, pertain to situations outside the present, in the future, the past, in the thoughts of others or in the reduced awareness of drifting. When these thoughts leave the present, they will be negative. Emotional reaction will follow these thoughts and will also be negative. By performing the Four Points, you are ensuring that a greater proportion of your thoughts pertain to the current environment thereby providing the structure of reality. As a result, your thoughts are more accurate

133

concerning the present environment and your emotional reaction will be appropriate, given the situation at hand. Try to keep value or importance realistic. Try to be accurate in your perception of reality. Think slowly and deliberately.

Fabricated high value has a disastrous effect on intelligence and can generate symptoms quite rapidly. Value is placed on events in reality by the intelligence. The value assigned to an item by your intelligence will depend on its relation to you and can be positive or negative. For instance, a family member is of higher value to you than a stranger. Or, your boss's negative impression if your report is late is more important to you than the opinion of a person whom you meet once and will probably never see again.

On the other hand, the habit has no intelligence; it cannot place value on items. Its sole purpose is to eliminate expression. To the habit, all events are a straight line, having no more or less value than any other. It will use the value your intelligence places on an event, situation, person, or condition against you to distract your attention and generate symptoms, all to prevent expression of taste. Situations, events, conditions and persons the habit attaches to will be taken as more serious the greater the awareness is diverted from the environment. The result is more intense symptoms.

Relapse from illness, fatigue or high value can be of short or long duration. Sometimes you will experience a short, intense anxiety. I call these relapses surges. Since the bad habit remains intact, it will exist below your awareness. The reason that you may rarely notice it is that its attempts to gain intensity are fended off by the new habit and your intelligence, thinking it stupid to out-of-control think. Every now and then, the bad habit may reach intensity during a gap or lapse in awareness. At these times, you will experience anxiety. The surge is brief and the new habit and your intelligence rapidly reduce its effect. The only time a surge will last longer is when you focus attention on it. Surges fade over time as the new habit gains strength and the bad habit atrophies or dismantles from disuse.

Most frequently, relapses occur when you forget to be focused and aware. These relapses generally occur in the beginning of Attention Training and as a result of resistance to the Four Points from the bad habit. Forgetting to perform the Four Points or regarding them lightly makes the mind fertile for the habit to attach to situations, influence the intelligence to place high value and generate symptoms. You experience an out-of-control thought or some other symptom and you pay attention to it, giving it more energy and power. The more attention you pay and the longer you attend to the symptom the deeper inside your head you are pulled, and the more intense the symptoms you will experience. As you lose more attention from the environment, your intelligence will become weaker and less able to fight the relapse, allowing it to last longer.

Once again, the easiest way to prevent a relapse is to consciously do the Four Points before you lose your attention. If you are consciously focused, you won't be able to relapse. Don't pay attention to out-of-control thoughts or other symptoms. Should you have a symptom, turn away from it, focus out, and increase your awareness of the environment.

GROGGINESS

A condition that many of my patients complain about concerns mornings. They tell me as soon as they open their eyes, they are hit with out-of-control thoughts and other symptoms that frequently set the tone for the entire day and make leaving the house difficult.

I refer to this fatigue problem as grogginess. Grogginess is the time between waking and full arousal. During grogginess, you will be inside your head experiencing symptoms. The idea is to reduce grogginess so you will be fully aroused and alert sooner. When you wake up in the morning, unless you intend to fall back to sleep, pop out of bed. Don't linger or you may be prone to out-of-control thoughts. Take a shower and feel the water. Turn on the radio, hear the music, and poke your head out the window. Stimulate your senses to reduce the period of grogginess. A few days of stimulating your senses in the morning will help reduce the effects of the habit upon awakening. If you build a strong new habit, mornings will no longer be a problem.

MEDICAL CONDITIONS

Medical conditions, other than illnesses, deserve some special attention in relation to their effect on your energy level and the possibility of relapse. Two medical conditions which have been treated in a most cruel and rude manner are Premenstrual Syndrome or PMS and menstruation. These conditions have been the center of jokes, blamed for differences of opinion, and used as justification for avoidance of communication and activity. The emotional discomfort resulting from PMS and menstruation has been seen in many women as a condition that cannot be avoided. I see the emotional discomfort as two conditions. The first is the normal, periodic precondition of menstruation and the menstrual cycle. Although not an illness, the change in the woman's body absorbs energy. She may feel physical discomfort and energy reduction. The second condition is the bad habit, triggered as a result of the woman's reduced energy. With reduced energy, irritability is pronounced, as is out-of-control thinking, anxiety, and depression.

Many of my female patients complained of the symptoms that accompanied PMS and menstruation. However, after Attention Training was completed, many of the additional symptoms experienced as a result of the bad habit were eliminated. All that was left were the symptoms produced directly from the conditions of PMS and menstruation.

The same is true for other medical conditions. One of my male patients was involved in an accident and as a result, lost his left arm. The pain that George experienced in cold, damp weather kept him home and in bed. George was part of an Attention Training experimental group that I conducted in Belmar. The winters on the Jersey shore are quite damp and chilly. As a result, George would have good mornings but discomfort in his shoulder would begin by noon. He would finally spend the rest of the day in bed, developing terrible pain by early evening.

I spoke with the psychologist whom he visited at the pain clinic and who described the techniques being used to help distract him from his pain. I told George that the techniques were standard and asked him to develop the new habit so we could rid him of the bad habit's ability to distract him from expression. I informed him that although the techniques used at the pain clinic would distract him from his pain, the distraction would only be temporary. Attention Training would develop a style of awareness that would prevent the bad habit from using his pain as a distraction from the present. As a result, George would be faced with his real pain and not the additional discomfort resulting from the attention that was being paid to his condition. By session five, George reported his pain was occurring much later in the day. This trend continued as he developed the new habit. By the time Attention Training was completed, George was suffering his pain by mid-evening. He had much of the day to witness the environment and we were able to conclude the remaining pain he suffered had a physical origin and was not the result of the bad habit. The rest was up to his physicians.

It's the same for any other physical insult or problem. The goal of Attention Training is to rid the individual of the influence of the bad habit so we may be left with only the discomfort related directly to the physical injury. The remaining discomfort may be dealt with medically and with a clearer vision of what is wrong and what may be accomplished.

LACK OF INFORMATION

Lack of information is one of the major sources for relapse. Without accurate information, out-of-control thinking can go rampant. I ask my patients not to draw conclusions concerning any event or situation without enough information. Some of these events and situations include medical conditions, what others may think, the past, and, of course, the future.

MONITORING YOUR ENERGY LEVEL

Relapses occur as a result of reduced energy. Whether the pressure is due to illness, a medical condition, fatigue, or high value, they all result in decreased energy levels. An excellent idea is to consciously monitor your energy level at all times. If you're fatigued or ill, slow down, don't expend so much energy. And, of course, don't take things too seriously. Although it must be done consciously for a time, monitoring your energy level will become automatic. You will notice you will no longer "push out" energy to handle situations but, instead, slow down. You will become more deliberate in your attention and focus and will handle one thing at a time. In other words, you will become more efficient in your energy use, especially when your energy is low.

RELATIONSHIPS WITH PEOPLE

Since the bad habit is often learned from criticism of expression during childhood, it may be seen as a social habit. Social interaction and situations are the greatest source for relapse. We are very concerned about what others think of us and we try to live our lives in a socially acceptable manner, following the rules of behavior and attempting to attain the goals others see as important. As a result, it is important you understand what you may expect from social situations as you begin to live life with the new habit.

With greater awareness of the environment, you will see many people with the bad habit. You will see it in friends, relatives, neighbors, and strangers. The bad habit is quite prevalent. You will see people who have difficulty making decisions, expressing opinions, or saying "no." They will tend to take differences personally and even see you as aggressive because you're expressive. Your job is not to allow their out-of-control thoughts and behaviors to trigger your bad habit. Don't give people and their thoughts too high a value.

However, there are some techniques and points that are important in your relationships with people. You will find you are unable to engage in avoidant behaviors as you once had. You will speak more directly with people and, over time, those with whom you are close will communicate with you more directly since you no longer accept indirect, avoidant communication.

Your new habit and the bad one in those around you will require that you <u>restructure your relationships</u> with some friends and relatives. For example, I have some friends with whom I will go to the movies but not to dinner, others with whom I will go to dinner but not to a dance club and still others with whom I will go to a dance club but not to the movies or to dinner. I am familiar with my taste and understand some of the people whom I know have different tastes than my own. As a result of restructuring your activities with those with whom you are close, you and they will enjoy each other's company to the fullest.

The same is so with different attitudes and values between you and others. I have friends and relatives with whom I will not discuss certain matters. I realize we see some things differently and discussion of these topics will only serve to have our time together less pleasurable than it could be. By restructuring relationships with those for whom you care, you are maximizing your interaction and, therefore, your relationship with the people whom you value.

There will be times when you are in situations where miscommunication leads to conflict. A technique you will find useful is <u>clarification</u>. If you are not certain of a person's meaning, ask her to clarify or to make the point clearer. The same is true if you are not sure your point is understood. You may ask if you have been clear and may restate your point for clarity.

Should you find yourself in a discussion that is leading to conflict, try to change the subject. Often, you will be aware of the direction of the discussion and the potential for conflict as a result of your knowledge of the person and your taste.

If you should find yourself in a discussion with a person who uses anger as an avoidant behavior, try to leave the discussion and save your time and energy. If you can't and your attempts to change the topic fail, be as neutral in your <u>communication</u> as you can. Should the person express offense with you, plead ignorance and apologize for any remark that offended, without admitting intention. Don't return the anger since this will only serve to justify the person's anger and create discomfort in you that is completely unnecessary.

At times, the angry person can make most techniques impossible to perform. They want to be angry and justify their avoidance of expression by pointing out how you and others offend them. Now it's time to do battle. Again, don't get angry in return. Instead, innocently question the perception of offense. Don't question in an accusatory way but in a helpful, benevolent manner. Apologize if you must, always without admitting intent. This technique is intended to disarm angry people because you are so nice about the incident. The angry person will then have two alternatives, to admit a mistake was made and to drop the matter or to remain angry. Should he choose to remain angry, politely excuse yourself from the conversation and try not to have contact with the person in the future.

However, there will be times when you will continue to have contact with angry people. They may be relatives, friends, co-workers, neighbors, or others. In this case, simply use the restructuring techniques. Stay away from conversation with content that usually leads to conflict. Keep away from situations that are less structured and, therefore, allow a wide range of topics and discussions, which may lead to conflict. Remove yourself from conversation where conflict appears inevitable. The emphasis is on prevention. Restructuring your relationships with angry people will generally allow you to maintain contact with these individuals without the upset of conflict.

A good rule to keep in mind is to use as few words as possible when expressing your opinion. This technique helps you to express directly and to the point. It also restricts misinterpretation from those with whom you relate.

There are certain behaviors that should raise a red flag when you see them. The first is controlling, manipulative behaviors. Should someone use indirect communication in an attempt to have you behave in a specific manner, be cautious. If the person isn't direct with you, pull back. The chances are they are attempting to manipulate you. A <u>manipulation</u> is an indirect request for a benefit from you. Some manipulations are guilt trips, intimidations, and the promise of a favor in the future. The manipulative person attempts to maneuver and control your behavior. When you meet one, don't waste your time getting angry, simply don't play the game.

The second behavior to be aware of is dependency. Dependency and a request for help can be confusing. <u>Help</u> is a mature request for assistance from a person who is temporarily unable to perform a function on her own. By all means, help her and those who require assistance. On the other hand, <u>dependency</u> occurs when a person who is capable of performing a function for himself attempts to maneuver and manipulate you to do the function for him. The dependent person pleads helplessness as the manipulation. If, in your judgment, a person is capable, let him fend for himself.

The discussion concerning social contact brings us to a fact that may initially upset you. As a result of your development of the new habit, the number of people with whom you may be close will decrease. This does not mean you will become isolated or antisocial, but you will be able to spot the habit in others and will be more selective with whom you associate. This is a difference from the past when you might be dissatisfied with a relationship because of the symptoms you and another may have displayed, causing you to blame yourself for any difficulty in the interaction. Now, you will be aware of your taste and how satisfying a relationship with another individual can be.

You will find that the people around you will notice a change in you. They may not be able to figure it out, but they will see you as different, in a positive way. Those who interact with you on an ongoing basis will tend to be more expressive since it is the behavior that you now accept. You will not be able to avoid expression. You will enjoy accomplishment and will look to handle situations and to help others.

These techniques worked for my patients as well as did the earlier ones. They added the structure of situations to the Four Points and awareness. As a result, all responded well to the intervention. They were happier and were not experiencing the terrible symptoms that plagued them when we first met. By 1990, I felt confident that the theory of Reflexive Attention Diversion and the technique of Attention Training had been completed. I was using the technique with all of my patients regardless of background, symptoms, or any other differences and with the same result, all improved. As long as the individual did not display a potential for harm, he received Attention Training.

From the first session, the individual was introduced to the theory of the habit and the Four Points. They were asked to be oriented, use their senses, to be active and to not drift and to only have on their minds what was hitting their senses. Patients were returning for their second session improved. By the fifth session, most had been able to reduce their symptoms dramatically. They weren't done, we needed to have the new habit become totally automatic, but they and I were amazed with the results of Attention Training.

I was seeing patients from late morning to ten or eleven o'clock at night. Referrals were coming from past and current patients and from doctors in psychiatry, psychology, internal medicine, and other specialties. My psychiatrist friend, Jim, sent me his most difficult patients who were not responding to medication. He would tell them he wasn't sure how I did it, but I got results. After I had a session or two with his patients, Jim would call me and compliment me on the change he noted.

It was unbelievable. I saw patients with all kinds of problems and was helping them to improve in a few sessions. I began seeing groups of patients with different problems, with the same result. The groups, like individual sessions, were not conducted around the patients' past or what was happening in their lives. All that was discussed was the bad habit and Attention Training.

By 1991, all my patients were doing well. Sandy was finally driving again. He was engaging in all sorts of activities and was largely symptom-free. He was down to an appointment once a month. Later in the year, I discharged him from treatment.

It was around this time that I stopped calling my people "patients." They weren't sick or ill. The problem wasn't in their minds but in their bodies. I wasn't treating them, I was teaching them. They were actually students, taking a course to learn what caused their symptoms and what to do about it. I simply began to call them "my people."

I knew I had developed a technique that was thought of as impossible in the field. All the people whom I saw received the same technique and improved. My thoughts began to turn toward how I would present the theory and technique to the profession. I knew others in the field would resist my theory as simplistic and impossible, but it had to be shared for the benefit of those who suffered symptoms.

However, designing research and presenting my theory to the field needed to be put off for a while. By the beginning of 1992, some of my people returned with their old symptoms battering them as if they had never met me or learned to focus. I had finished with some of them as long as four years earlier and they had left me with their new habit strong and in control. So why did they relapse so severely?

This was a major setback that had me confused and quite concerned.

Chapter VIII

Taking Back Small Times

---

*"Another thing we should remark is the grace and fascination that there
is even in the incidentals of Nature's process."*
Marcus Aurelius

I was devastated. Some of the people who had left Attention
Training feeling better than ever in their lives came back to me in
the same condition as they were when I first met them. They told
me they had felt wonderful when they left me and slowly, over
approximately two years for most, the habit returned fully and with
the same intensity as it had prior to their seeing me initially.

I was confused. The new habit was strong when each of them
left, and I thought it would continue at the same strength for the
rest of their lives. I couldn't understand how the bad habit could
return with such intensity. None of them had experienced a trauma
or an unusual event that could account for the relapse. So what
could it be?

I had each of them begin the Four Points as they had when I
first met them. To my amazement, all were back to feeling excellent
after only two or three sessions. This was important information for
me. What it meant was the new habit was still in their bodies. By
having each do the Four Points, we actually "jump started" the new
habit and it kicked in, reducing the bad one back to its previous
dormant status.

For some reason, my people and their bodies stopped using the
new habit and had relapsed. This question stumped me for a while
and then it dawned on me. The Four Points worked to build the
new habit by using big events like clouds, wind, trees, music, food
and so on. But what about the times between events, when activity
and surroundings were not so attractive and big? What about these

144

"small times?" Upon questioning my people, I found that there were times when they were not using the Four Points. I refer to these instances as <u>small times</u>, the time between two events. For example, you get up from the couch and go to the refrigerator. The walk was a small time. You come home from work and, as you kiss your spouse hello, you place your keys on the mantle. Placing your keys on the mantle is a small time. I found that many of my people might forget what they went to the refrigerator for or where they had placed their keys. I realized that these small times had something to do with the reason why my people relapsed.

It seemed logical that the bad habit gained strength at times when my people weren't aware. I knew that they were doing the Four Points after they left intervention and me. So how could the bad habit gain sufficient strength to overpower the new one? It had to be during the small times between events that the bad habit was gaining strength. The inattention during small times didn't appear to be significant or dramatic. If it had been, my people would have noticed it since symptoms would have been generated. The fade of attention during small times had to be slight, but how could a slight fade cause a relapse? The answer had to be that the slight fade of attention accumulated over time. If that were true, the cumulative effect would eventually reach a level that would distract conscious thoughts and behaviors, producing an out-of-control attitude, which caused relapse.

I knew the new habit was built in my people's conscious thoughts through the Four Points. <u>Conscious thoughts</u> are the thoughts you are aware of and that direct your behavior. For instance, I am consciously typing on my computer. I consciously intend to type the next word and I am consciously attending to the screen to see if what I have written is what I intended. These are the thoughts that occur as a result of awareness. You consciously walk to the refrigerator for a cold drink. You intentionally change the TV channel to watch the Yankees at a certain time. You decide to buy your husband a video you know he wants. Conscious thoughts are purposeful. They reflect your taste and prompt you to behave for your benefit.

However, I realized there must be another variety of thought and behavior below conscious awareness where inattention during small times contributed to and fed the bad habit. The logic of this variety of thought led me to what I refer to as <u>orienting thoughts and behaviors</u>. Orienting thoughts are learned from birth and include skills and behaviors that occur in response to our perception of familiar situations, events, and conditions. Orienting thoughts are cognitive, or in the mind, and physical in their behavioral response, or in the body.

Over our lives, we learn information from familiar events that eventually become reflexive. Although we are not consciously aware of the information, it is there for us when we need it. The information may be brought to consciousness or be initiated automatically, without our awareness. I can bring some of this information to your consciousness simply by mentioning certain events to you. Ready? The taste of an orange, Easter Sunday, the summer, the way home from the supermarket, your car (if you have one), your family, Monday mornings, fried eggs, Europe, a red balloon, snow.

See what I mean? The information that came to awareness was not consciously on your mind before I brought it up. It became conscious when I mentioned it. What a marvelous mechanism. This means you can live your life with your own personal encyclopedia available to you whenever you may need some information. Even better, the same mechanism works in the body. So we can walk and talk at the same time, catch a ball that's thrown by surprise, scratch our arm as we read a book, sit comfortably, reach for a door knob and turn it as we look at a grocery list, or think and have words automatically convey our thoughts through speech, etc. Orienting thoughts and behaviors are wonderful mechanisms that make living easier, but where do they come from?

Over time, the body and mind learn information necessary to accomplish certain familiar tasks and, with repetition, they become automatic. They are triggered when we perceive situations that call for their assistance. You can better understand orienting thoughts and behaviors if you equate them with other skills that you have acquired over the years. For example, if you found that you had an interest in baseball, you might practice hitting and catching to the point where the behaviors become automatic. Now, when a ball is hit to you in the field, you catch it automatically and throw it to first for the out. Another example is acquiring the skill to ride a bike. You weren't born with the knowledge; you tried riding with training wheels at first, then without. You had to concentrate. You needed to eliminate as much peripheral or surrounding information as you could and focus on attempting to maintain your balance. You'd fall, get up, fall, and get up again and, after enough repetitions, your body learned balance and you rode your bicycle.

However, let's say you're fifty-two years old and you haven't been on a bicycle for twenty-five years. You're at a friend's house and he takes out a couple of bicycles. You get on the bike cautiously. After some stiffness, you ride the bike without falling. The balance that allowed you to ride the bike at fifty-two is the same balance that you learned when you were a kid. It was triggered and came into operation when you needed it.

I saw an example of orienting thoughts and behaviors last summer. I watched a father and mother with their young daughter. The girl was about one-and-a-half years old and was walking back and forth between them. The girl was delighted with the behavior, as were her parents who rewarded her with smiles and expressions, both verbal and behavioral. What I saw was the girl practicing a behavior that would eventually become a response to an orienting thought. Later in life, the girl will walk spontaneously while looking at the sky, talking with friends, shopping, moving toward the front door and so on.

Orienting thoughts and their accompanying behaviors provide a sort of backdrop for conscious thoughts and behaviors. Because orienting thoughts involve reflexive responses and behaviors in reaction to familiar situations, they are quite economical. The body doesn't have to waste energy attending to them. This leaves more energy to devote to conscious thoughts and behaviors for your benefit and enjoyment.

An example of orienting thoughts and behaviors is buying French fries on the boardwalk at Seaside Heights (a New Jersey seashore town). You are able to be oriented so you know where you are, stand at the counter, speak, and order what you want, pay for the fries, count your change, and walk away without losing touch with your direction and destination. Most of the behaviors mentioned, aside from your conscious decision to approach a counter to buy French fries, were the result of orienting thoughts and behaviors. Even speaking, besides what you consciously intend to say, is the result of orienting thoughts and behaviors. You decide what you want to communicate and the words flow out, making for a very economical interaction with your surroundings.

Another example is leaving the present to plan a future event. Let's say you and a friend are planning a vacation. You are both really into it and your thoughts are engrossed with images of the sea, sun, sand, and palm trees. With the plan set, your thoughts return to the present, you automatically resume your routine, without a thought of confusion, and you didn't miss a beat. Or, let's say that you're really focused on the computer. You're playing a game or something that really has your total interest. The phone rings with an important call that you were expecting. Amazingly, your conscious thoughts turn toward the phone. You know the time of day, your responsibilities for the day, who is in the house and what the call is probably about. When the call is completed, you pick up the game where you left off.

As you can see, orienting thoughts and behaviors keep you anchored in time and place. They contain all the information you require in order to place you at the specific point in your life where you were before your conscious thoughts traveled to another place in time (planning the future), or focused on a specific event (the computer), to the exclusion of the events which were occurring around you.

Can you imagine how difficult life would be if every time you left your house and went to the store you had to figure out how to return home? Or, if you wanted to ask for directions, you had to relearn how to speak and which words to use. Or, for that matter, even after you had received directions as to how to return home, you had to figure out how to walk. Truly, orienting thoughts and their reflexive behaviors are a blessing that we could not live without.

There are situations when some orienting thoughts are closer to consciousness. For instance, I'm more aware of my orienting thoughts while I'm typing because I'm more focused on an activity that requires both conscious and orienting thoughts and behaviors. If you're playing pinball or a video game, you might realize that your conscious attention, as well as your reflexes, are coordinated in order to score well.

However, there are situations where you might not be as aware of your orienting thoughts. These situations are ones that don't require much of your participation. Some are talking on the phone, watching TV, reading a book, walking from your car to the house, getting up in the morning, reaching for a pen, driving your car and so on. While you were engaged in these activities, you were automatically oriented to your surroundings, less consciously aware of where you were and what was going on around you. Should something have occurred that needed your attention, your orienting thoughts and behaviors would have automatically directed your attention toward that situation and you would have behaved for your benefit. This is the reason why we are able to be in a busy situation like work, and also able to handle so many things, seemingly, at once.

Orienting thoughts and behaviors don't require much attention. Because of that, it seemed to me, if there were a problem that caused my people to relapse, it would have to involve orienting thoughts and behaviors. Although I realized the inattention during small times was actually an avoidant behavior, I also understood it was a short step for these behaviors to disturb the function of orienting thoughts and behaviors. I knew the bad habit resisted expression on a conscious level. If you're in a situation to express, such as saying "no" to a request from someone or doing what you want, the bad habit clobbers you with anxiety. The Four Points worked very well on conscious thoughts, but it's logical that orienting thoughts also contain your taste. You walk in a manner that's comfortable. You like sunny days rather than rainy ones. You like apples rather than oranges. You sit with one leg under the other because it feels comfortable when you're typing. You like scrambled rather than fried eggs. Although both contain your taste, you're more aware of conscious thoughts and less aware of many orienting thoughts and not at all of others.

Since both conscious and orienting thoughts contain your taste, it is logical to assume that the bad habit would constrict orienting thoughts as it does conscious ones. If this was true, and since the Four Points works only on conscious thoughts, then it was possible for the bad habit to gain strength in my people's orienting thoughts, eventually distracting their conscious thoughts and causing relapse.

It appeared that symptoms from the bad habit created a chronic and constant discomfort, on a reflexive level, within the individual's orienting thoughts and behaviors. Although my people had not experienced symptoms with any intensity, over time the effect was cumulative, and they relapsed. It seemed when the bad habit reached a level of intensity in the individual's orienting thoughts and behaviors; the discomfort was experienced on a conscious level. The result was that out-of-control thoughts were generated and symptoms were produced.

I understood that the bad habit worked directly against conscious thoughts, distracting attention from the environment in order to prevent expression. But orienting thoughts are subtler. The bad habit had to negate expression in orienting thoughts on a reflexive level. It would eliminate the style that affects all your behavior. There would be the same guardedness and over-vigilance against the bad thing on a reflexive level as occurred in conscious thoughts and behaviors. This would explain why you jump when the phone rings or when you startle awake as you're drifting off to sleep. It would also explain the tightness in your muscles, which you had been unaware of until you felt it in your arms, legs or in the back of the neck. The bad habit in your orienting thoughts may also be responsible for your chronic upset stomach, your sleep problems, the awkwardness and the tightness you feel in your movement whether you're around people or alone at home, as well as the nervousness and anxiety you feel when you have free time and can do what you want.

A disruption in your orienting thoughts and behaviors would be devastating, leaving you confused about where you are and what's going on around you. With the habit causing holdback in your orienting thoughts and behaviors, your conscious thoughts experience confusion.

Some of my people have reported feeling a deep down, underneath awareness, tension, and nervousness while they are focused using the Four Points. They were specific in describing that it was not anxiety from negative thinking and that they were very focused and feeling in control when they had this feeling. They told me that the feeling was shakiness from deep inside, beneath their intelligence and their feelings. My reaction was that this "deep down" anxiety was due to the bad habit in my people's orienting thoughts.

It made sense to me that the bad habit existed on a reflexive level and that in order for my people to be successfully free from its influence, the new habit would have to be developed in their orienting thoughts and behaviors. The problem was how to do it. How could we develop the new habit in an individual's orienting thoughts and behaviors since she was largely unaware of their presence?

The Four Points worked well to have a person feel pleasure as the result of increased awareness. With repetition, a habit is created which seeks pleasure from increased awareness while disallowing pain from the bad habit. It seemed I could use the same process with orienting thoughts.

This problem was on my mind through 1992. By the end of the year, I thought I had it figured out. I needed to find a way to convert at least some orienting thoughts and behaviors to conscious ones. I could pair them with the pleasure of awareness and the body would generalize the pleasure and the new habit to all orienting thoughts and behaviors. But how could I do it?

I instructed my people to be aware of peripheral information (the events which were occurring around them) that they wouldn't ordinarily notice. I asked them to be aware of the walk from the couch to the refrigerator, to watch themselves place the keys on the table, to be aware of what is going on around them as they looked at the newspaper. However, I soon realized a problem with the technique. What if, when my people attended to peripheral information, they simply diverted their conscious thoughts to the information? All we would accomplish was to redirect the Four Points to other events. This would mean that the bad habit would remain in the body, continuing to affect orienting thoughts and behaviors on a reflexive level and eventually causing relapse. I needed to find a way to work on orienting thoughts and behaviors independent of conscious ones.

After much thought, I believed I had figured it out. I asked my people to expand their awareness of peripheral information as much as they could while they were consciously focused on what they were doing. For instance, as I'm focused on my writing, I'm aware of hearing Montel Williams on TV talking about amnesia. I hear the wind outside, building momentum and fading. I can feel the floor beneath my feet and the pressure of the chair's edge on my thighs. I can feel the keys beneath my fingers as I tap them. I can see the wall to my right and the windows in front of me, and to my left. I can feel my body as I move and even feel my eyes blink. All the time that I'm aware of peripheral information, I have maintained my focus on my work. My awareness of small times is in addition to my conscious focus. It's not like I'm consciously focusing on what's going on around me and where I am, I'm simply aware that I know where I am.

A great example of how orienting thoughts work came from Will. I had completed Attention Training with Will in 1994. Will was dedicated to the Four Points, and as a result his anxiety attacks decreased to zero and he was discharged. I was just beginning to teach my people the technique of taking back small times when Will left intervention.

Recently, Will made an appointment with me. His anxiety attacks had returned and he was upset. He told me he had practiced the Four Points every day since he left me in 1994 but now his anxiety was back and felt horrible. Will lasted the longest of my people before relapse after using the Four Points. I believe that it was using the Four Points daily that had Will last the six years before he relapsed.

There's no way a person should have to perform the Four Points constantly. Awareness was to be automatic, not allowing decreased attention, out-of-control thoughts, and anxiety. Will's story pointed to the flaw in Attention Training during the mid-90's. The problem for Will was I didn't have taking back small times perfected when he left me.

The first thing Will and I needed to do was to stop him from "looking over his shoulder" to see if the habit was gaining on him, ready to clobber him with terrible thoughts and horrible anxiety. We used the Four Points to reduce his cautiousness. When Will increased his attention and awareness, he found himself more in the present, in a sort of "safety-zone," where the habit couldn't hurt him.

With his anxiety under control, Will and I began taking back small times. He had no trouble understanding the technique but found it difficult to perform. Will's problem was that he tended to focus on orienting thoughts and behaviors rather than simply be aware of where he was and what was going on around him. Taking back small times should be like knowledge in the back of your mind, a thought as to where you are, the time of day and what's going on around you.

It took Will four sessions, but he began to get it. We were sitting in my Jersey City office and talking about small times. Will mentioned, that while he focused on me and on our conversation, he heard a car horn filter into the room. He didn't focus on the horn, interpret it or decrease his attention toward me. He was simply aware of it as he was of my office, being in Jersey City, the time of day and the rest of his surroundings.

His next description was important and demonstrates the difference between more and less awareness of orienting thoughts. Will said, without taking back small times, the sound of the horn might well have had him initially believe that he was in a traffic jam, with the driver at his rear, leaning on the horn for Will to stop his daydreaming and move his vehicle, causing him to be alarmed that he had done something "wrong."

Will's description accurately portrays the role of the bad habit in your orienting thoughts and behaviors. The same tension and cautiousness that exists in your conscious thoughts and behaviors can be found in your orienting ones. A return of your conscious thoughts to the present is immediately met with a signal that "something may be wrong" in the current. On a conscious level, the intelligence problem-solves the discomfort and misinterprets the available information as negative, and a state of alarm is triggered. In Will's case, he got the driver behind him angry because he did something "wrong." He wasn't moving fast enough in traffic. All this could have taken place as he sat in my office if he hadn't been taking back small times.

During his last session, Will told me he was in a traffic jam on the Turnpike, a situation that would ordinarily cause him anxiety. I asked him why he didn't become anxious and he said, "Because I knew I was on the Turnpike." He got it. He told me he automatically knew where he was and the same tendency to be automatically oriented maintained throughout the week. It made no difference whether he was at home, work, walking in the park or driving. Will automatically knew where he was and what was going on around him. This is taking back small times. By having Will begin with conscious attention to peripheral information, he eventually taught his body to be aware of time, place, and surroundings automatically. The result was that his orienting thoughts and behaviors kept him anchored to reality without confusion.

From our discussion and Will's example, it is easy to see just how important orienting thoughts and behaviors are for our comfort. They help us to interact with the environment in a smooth manner, allowing us to be economical in our behavior so that we can accomplish more with our day and in our lives.

The purpose of taking back small times is to develop from a point of awareness of peripheral information to one of an attitude or style of thinking that includes all peripheral information at once. For instance, my knowledge of where I am (at home) includes a knowledge of the lay of the house, the time of day, the refrigerator motor running, the sounds and the feel of my house and all other aspects that are common to my home. With this knowledge on an orienting thought and behavior level, the phone may ring without startling me. I would simply turn from my computer, answer the phone, and then resume my work from where I left off. This was the case when Will knew he was on the Turnpike. His knowledge of where he was included the time of day, day of the week and his purpose for being there. With this orienting information available instantaneously, Will was unable to become anxious as he had in the past.

With small times accomplished, the new habit will automatically keep you oriented to time and place. Even gaps in awareness will be filled by the new habit so that surges will reduce in frequency and finally, not occur at all.

It is important you understand that the Four Points must be mastered before you begin taking back small times. Learning the Four Points will have you understand attentiveness, focusing, and awareness. This will set you up for taking back small times.

At the office, I teach my people the Four Points first. Even with the larger items like clouds and wind to focus conscious thoughts, my people have some difficulty understanding attention and awareness. If I were to begin intervention with taking back small times, I would totally confuse them and render the intervention useless. The same is true for you. Start with the easier, more concrete Four Points. Once your conscious thoughts are focused on the environment automatically so that out-of-control thoughts are no longer a problem, then you can begin taking back small times. Be smart. Do it right the first time.

Clearly, the Four Points and taking back small times are two separate techniques. The Four Points is intended to extend attention and therefore, awareness. Taking back small times is intended to expand your awareness. It's logical that if you have an extended and expanded awareness, it would be just about impossible to have an out-of-control thought.

My people had some difficulty understanding taking back small times and more difficulty accomplishing the procedure. The problem they had was getting familiar with attending to more than one thing at a time. Each experienced similar problems with taking back small times as they had when first attempting the Four Points. Resistance from the bad habit had them forget to perform the procedure just as it did with the Four Points. However, after two or three weeks of faithful persistence, they reported the technique was becoming easier. Most importantly, their rates of progress increased dramatically.

Asking all my people to practice taking back small times brought nothing but success. Some needed to be pushed a bit as a result of resistance, but all progressed at an outstanding rate. It made sense. The theory hadn't changed at all. Symptoms had to do with a decrease of awareness toward the environment. Although the Four Points was completely logical and reduced symptoms almost immediately, it was necessary to develop the new habit on a reflexive level, in orienting thoughts and behaviors.

This was it. It was amazing. Not only did my people feel better, they looked better. Tense, anxious, depressed, angry people look tense, anxious, depressed, and angry. Relaxed people look relaxed. When symptoms were removed, my people looked physically better. They were more attractive. They looked calm, warm, and friendly.

Some time in 1992 and before I discovered taking back small times, Sandy was discharged. He was great. He was going out, driving, and having fun, all without symptoms. True, the bad habit would attempt to distract him, but Sandy wouldn't look at the thoughts. He was doing very well.

Sandy had been with me through the development of Attention Training. I needed to contact him and tell him of small times. I called Sandy and had him come in. He understood the concept and promised he would perform the procedure and call if he had any trouble. Sandy checked in with me periodically and explained he was doing well and had no problem with taking back small times.

By the end of 1994, the Four Points and taking back small times were developed to the point that I was teaching them to all my people without any problem at all. I generally spent little time taking down background information, a procedure that requires several sessions in more traditional treatment. From the first session, so long as the person was not physically harmful to himself or to others, I would teach the sequence of the bad habit and instruct the person as to how to perform the Four Points. Many asked me how I knew what they were going through, and my answer would always be the same, "That's how all people work."

Most of my people had seen other doctors prior to coming to me and were accustomed to relating their histories. I would discourage this and would get right to the explanation of the bad habit, how it developed, and the Four Points. If any of my people needed to speak of situations, I would certainly allow it, but I would speak of the situation from the point of view of the habit and Attention Training. All would leave the first session hopeful and motivated. This was the first time any had received a logical explanation for their symptoms. Now they understood the source for their discomfort and had tools they could use against the habit and the symptoms it generated. The course of the intervention was mostly the same for all of my people. Three to five weeks to develop the new habit through the Four Points, with instruction as to how to perform taking back small times somewhere around the fourth or fifth session. Most individuals were completed, symptom-free and in the present, with reflexive awareness within ten to fifteen sessions.

By 1995, the techniques were working really well. I was seeing all kinds of people with all kinds of problems. I was asking them fewer questions pertaining to their symptoms and streamlining the intervention. Other doctors were sending their hard to treat patients to me and these people were responding to my Attention

Training almost immediately. To their doctors' surprise, they would return for medication evaluation with reduced symptoms.

Because Attention Training is not personal, I didn't need to search my people's thoughts, secrets, pasts, or fantasies. There was no question of breaking confidentiality. I was able to see individuals from the same families and their friends as well. As a result, I would see clusters of people who knew each other. Often these people would discuss the techniques on their own, outside of our sessions. In one instance, I was seeing three brothers in the same time frame. They had different problems and were seen for individual sessions. All received Attention Training, all progressed, and all were discharged with the new habit and symptom-free.

Finally, the theory was perfected. It was simple, to the point, and answered many of the questions concerning psychological discomfort. I anticipated that I would be ready to share the intervention with the profession and the public by the end of 2000. I had extreme confidence in Attention Training. It had proven itself over and over again with the most difficult people and symptoms. Now psychology could be as predictable as any medical procedure. There was no need for people to suffer the terrible symptoms as they had in the past.

Chapter IX

The Finished Product

"Try to see, before it is too late, that you have within you something higher and more godlike than mere instincts which move your emotions and twitch you like a puppet."
Marcus Aurelius

With the new habit developed in your conscious and orienting thoughts, symptoms are virtually gone. Should you experience any anxiety at all, it will be as a surge, when your attention lapses. Remember, we have not replaced the bad habit; we have built a new habit. As a result, the bad habit attempts to gain dominance but cannot because of resistance from the new habit and logic from intelligence.

The good news is that instances of surges will decrease over time as the new habit continues to strengthen and the bad habit dismantles or atrophies. You will notice that out-of-control thoughts are at a minimum. Should you have any, your new habit and intelligence will blow them away. It will become literally "stupid" for you to worry or attend to negative thoughts.

Your expression, or interaction with the environment, will be spontaneous. Your movement will be fluid and economical, you will say what you mean, and your thoughts will pertain to what is occurring in the environment. You will be decisive according to your taste. You will not take differences of opinion personally as offensive acts, but will properly see them as points of view. The only time you will do what you may not want will be out of consideration for others whom you value.

Sensory perception will be sharper than ever before. You will notice birds singing, the color of flowers, clouds in the sky, the sound of children playing and all sorts of things happening around you that you hadn't noticed when you were inside your head thinking negatively.

Your relationships with people will become closer and more fun. You will not be able to feel threat as you once had. You will understand that all, including you, are entitled to an opinion and you will not be offended by differences. You will not take responsibility for behaviors that are not yours. You will notice people will enjoy your company. They will like your expressive, accepting manner.

Physically, you will lose your tension. Your stomach will stop hurting and the chronic knot at the center of your back or your neck will vanish. Your sleep will improve, and you will awaken rested each morning. Most noticeably, you will have energy you have not felt since you can remember.

If you have used food as an inefficient activity and as a source of pleasure because you avoided socializing and engaging your taste, you will lose some weight. The reduction of the habit's influence on your thinking will allow you to become more active and to do the things you want. You won't stay in the house because you fear something may happen out there that you may not be able to handle. You will place emphasis on enjoying your interests rather than avoiding them.

You will finally have the confidence that you lacked most of your life. I define <u>confidence</u> as an automatic knowledge that you will be capable of handling any situation that may come your way. As a result, you will not worry about future events, since you know you will handle them as they occur.

We have all met and enjoyed confident people. They are in the present, social and happy and tend to make those around them comfortable. They don't out-of-control think and are focused in conversation and in their lives on what is occurring in the present. They have been raised to be expressive and not to take differences of opinion personally as angry acts. People with the new habit as a result of Attention Training will have the same confidence as those who were raised to be expressive. The only difference will be that

Attention Trained people will know where confidence exists; in the present.

Your thinking will be clear. You will be able to attend to and handle many items at one time without feeling overwhelmed. Your ability to concentrate and remember will be enhanced. You will be creative and the expression of your taste will develop into interests.

You will notice events that would upset you in the past have lost their power. As a matter of fact, you will not be able to understand how they could have upset you to begin with. You will take some events and situations as important but not serious. You will behave toward them efficiently and to the point, without holdback.

Best of all, the new habit will continue to develop. Since Attention Training is based on the Pleasure Principle, your body will literally seek stimulation and pleasure. This will ensure that the new habit will grow stronger over time. Although the bad habit exists fully in your body, its ability to be triggered will decrease as the new habit strengthens. Aside from surges, which you will ignore, you will not expect relapse. As time passes, influence from the bad habit will continue to decrease to the point where its effect will be zero.

Well, let's see how my people did. It's been some years, but I've heard from most and about some from new people who have been referred by them.

Jim still loves the Knicks although they continue to break his heart every year. Previously, his bad habit wouldn't allow him to fully enjoy himself. Jim doesn't suffer panic attacks any longer. He's an intelligent man who has taken what he learned and applied it. His motivation was the backbone of his change. He enjoys his family, engages in sports, has fun with his friends and is successful in business. It's been about six years since Jim and I completed his Attention Training.

What can I say about Sandy? It was his terrible symptoms that pushed me to develop Attention Training as quickly as I could. Here was a motivated young man who complied with all the procedures the doctors had prescribed. He took buses into New York City, took medications, searched his past, tried vitamins and diet changes. Sandy had seen a total of twelve doctors before he was referred to me.

He summarized his frustration with traditional treatment by telling me a story concerning a psychiatrist he had seen. Sandy had visited with the doctor for over two years. They both knew that the procedures were not working in Sandy's case. One day, Sandy arrived at the doctor's office for his scheduled appointment. He settled into his introspective manner, intent on investigating the content of his thoughts and their relationship to his hellish symptoms, in an attempt to reduce the crippling behaviors that effectively stopped him from living his life. Before Sandy could begin relating the week's events, the doctor began to speak. He told Sandy he had tried as best he could and felt very good concerning his efforts but had decided he couldn't help him. Sandy was silent but screamed inside his head, "You feel good. What about me?" Sandy quietly rose from his chair and left the doctor's office, not knowing where to look for help.

I felt much compassion for Sandy. He didn't deserve to endure the horrible symptoms that he experienced. He cooperated with my techniques and did well. He even visited me when I discovered small times. Sandy has always kept in touch with me. He even referred his sister, Roma, to me. Roma suffered from anxiety attacks when she was alone. Sandy told me about Roma years ago, but she was hesitant to meet me. Finally, she consented to try Attention Training. She has had eight sessions and hasn't had an anxiety attack since her third visit with me. Sandy even sits in during the last half of Roma's sessions and points out concepts about Attention Training that were important to him and how Roma may improve her techniques and skills as a result of his mistakes and experiences.

Sandy continues to do well. He drives his car wherever he wants, works, goes out, and suffers none of the avoidant behaviors that stopped him from living life in the past. I hope to be always in touch with Sandy.

Jenny looked frazzled when I met her. She was beside herself and she was scared. Initially, she resisted the theory and the Four Points, thinking them too simple to explain the severe symptoms she experienced. However, she agreed to try them and noticed that her symptoms decreased somewhat. Within weeks, her symptoms had diminished while her intelligence increased. She understood the thoughts that she would kill herself by drinking detergent or by some other means were her intelligence's attempt to identify the enemy. With Jenny, the habit fabricated that the "bad thing" within her would lead to her self-inflicted death.

Once she gained the new habit, Jenny intelligently understood that her taste was not harmful and she was entitled to her own taste and its expression for her happiness. It was like an invisible line that she crossed. Once her attention and awareness was increased, it was impossible for her to view expression of taste personally, as an angry act. Jenny completed Attention Training more than four years ago and hasn't even come close to a relapse. As she continues to live, her new habit will gain more and more strength. Jenny can't think in any other way but in the present.

When I met Sam, he had a stunned expression on his face, as if someone had whacked him on the forehead with a baseball bat. His anxiety was excruciating, and he was willing to try anything to stop it. Sam caught on rather quickly. He was able to see his compulsions and rituals as distractions from the present where he might express himself. Intervention with Sam went smoothly, and he completed Attention Training in a couple of months, around the fall of 1995. The key to Sam's rapid progress was his motivation. He was determined to get rid of his symptoms and live a happy life.

Sam continues to keep in touch. He bought me a steak dinner in Hoboken about two years ago and continues to call and visit every couple of months. Recently, Sam asked my advice on doctoral programs in psychology. Currently, he holds a Master's degree in clinical psychology and works at a group home for adolescents. I just learned that Sam was accepted into a doctoral program and will begin school this fall. I have no doubt Sam will become an excellent psychologist.

Bob was a recent case. He had no history of anxiety, depression or any other symptoms prior to his accident. Attention Training with someone like Bob is really quite easy. Because he had been expressive to begin with, Bob was able to have some frame of reference for developing the new habit. Most people whom I see have lived with the bad habit and the tendency to take differences of opinion personally throughout their entire lives. They don't know a different way to live. They literally need to learn a different style of thinking and behaving. Fortunately for Bob, he was able to readily understand the concept of focus and the function of out-of-control thoughts. He understood he needed to maintain awareness by paying more attention to the environment and by ignoring his symptoms. Bob required four sessions to regain his ability to drive, express, and be happy.

Bill was frightened by what the New York psychiatrist had told him concerning a biochemical imbalance and by the thought of a lifetime of medication. Bill worked as hard on Attention Training as he had on bodybuilding. He stopped using steroids and reduced his size. He soon lost his anxiety, depression, anger, and lack of confidence. He developed tactful expression as a result of understanding differences as points of view. He became considerate, attentive, patient and friendly. Attention Training for Bill lasted three months. He returned one time about two years later, in 1997. It wasn't a relapse or a symptom that brought him back. Bill wanted some advice concerning a woman he had met. Our conversation required one session.

I hadn't heard from Bill since that time until he sent his regards through a co-worker whom he referred to me in December 1999. Jack told me Bill was married, happy and feeling just fine.

Sarah didn't want to feel as she did. Although she initially resisted intervention, she performed the Four Points and did very well with them. Her major problem was getting hit by the bad habit during her free time when she could do as she liked. While the Four Points reduced her anxiety, taking back small times eliminated her holdback and allowed her to enjoy her free time. Her drinking decreased also. Although she is able to have a drink or two at social gatherings or a glass of wine with dinner, she simply prefers not to.

Sarah completed Attention Training in 1996. She and Tony married in 1998 and are quite happy together. Sarah has taken a leave of absence from her job because she is expecting. When she returns, she will work part time so she can spend more time at home with the baby.

Pat had tried other treatments before she came to me. Her basic problem, similar to Sandy's, was that she was a caretaker, putting aside her own taste and wants for those of others. She would have anxiety whenever she was close to doing what she wanted. Her anxiety attack while crossing the Raritan River Bridge effectively stopped her from visiting her family and created negative anticipation about leaving home. One interesting story Pat told me occurred while she was receiving behavioral treatment from a doctor in northern New Jersey. Under his direction, while in the doctor's office, Pat was able to imagine crossing a bridge without anxiety. During the next step, actually having Pat drive across a bridge with the doctor as a passenger, Pat froze at the top of a bridge on Route 3 at Secaucus. The doctor had to climb over Pat to take the wheel and drive off the bridge. Her attempt to drive over a bridge was simply too soon. Pat never returned to the doctor after the experience and came to me the very next week.

Pat worked hard on the Four Points and small times and progressed nicely over a four-month period. She needed some time to understand she could say "no" to her family and others. But once her new habit gained strength, Pat was able to express, even during differences with others.

Pat's fear of heights and of crossing bridges decreased over the course of Attention Training. She used the technique of leaning out with attention when she knew she was coming to a bridge or would need to ascend above the first floor of a building, and she was fine. Recently, she needed to visit her father on the fifth floor of a local hospital. She handled the situation with focus and no anxiety. Pat remains in touch and has had no problems with heights, bridges, expression, or symptoms since we ended her Attention Training in 1995.

Fran began intervention with me in early 1998. I saw some members of her family and a few of her friends who encouraged her to try Attention Training. She was anxious and depressed but was most concerned with her eating disorder. I didn't want Fran to lose too much more weight so I decided to see her twice a week. Fran caught on to Attention Training right away and worked the Four Points well. Her symptoms decreased nicely. Her gorging and purging reduced to my and her family's great relief.

The problem I had with Fran was having her remember to take back small times. Fran and I agreed to make an all out effort for her to remember to use the technique. Just before her next session, I left the office to get a file from my car. There was Fran, walking up the block. I walked toward her and my car. We passed each other without Fran noticing me. Fran and I talked about our problem during that session. We decided she would print post-ups and hang them where she would notice them as reminders to practice taking back small times.

The technique worked and Fran was taking back small times everywhere. She was aware of low stimulation situations and expanding her attention all the time. She leaned out toward the environment with attention and was particularly focused during meals and during her free time at night when she might eat junk food. She ate healthy and gained eight pounds. Fran was able to see she needed the weight to change her emaciated appearance.

Attention Training with Fran took nine months, a bit longer than usual. But Fran needed it. She needed to become independent of her mother and to make her own decisions. Fran learned to handle conflict with her mother well. She didn't feel guilty for expressing her opinion and didn't let her mother's bad habit trigger her own. I was very proud of Fran.

Although Fran experienced much resistance from the bad habit, she persisted. Fran wanted to be symptom-free and happy. Fran is married to an Englishman who wants to settle down with a wonderful wife and have children. I spoke with Fran about three months ago upon her return from a trip to visit her in-laws. Fran is quite happy.

Billy was difficult. He was referred to me by his internist in 1993. His father accompanied him to his appointments since I believed the man would be helpful in reminding Billy of the techniques to practice. Billy's Attention Training was painstaking for us both. The resistance he got from the bad habit was extreme. He would make progress but be pulled inside his head when a storm approached or his grandmother visited.

It took months and months, but Billy began to make steady progress. He got a job and was beginning to enjoy his free time. He described increased awareness as feeling like a "party." Billy's Attention Training was not completed when he had to move to Florida in 1995. I haven't heard from him but I hope he's doing well. I know he took all the notes he and I jotted down for him, so maybe he is.

I never saw Jerry for intervention. Jerry's a friend. Although I certainly would see a friend for Attention Training, it just never got there for Jerry and me. He was like a lot of people you see all the time. People who have trouble saying "no" or making decisions or who are overly concerned about doing the wrong thing. They don't have panic attacks, they just aren't as happy as they could be. They're not loose and free.

Jerry would often ask me questions about what I do and about the people whom I see. One time I decided to sit him down and explain the habit and Attention Training to him. Jerry made good use of our discussion. I noticed a change in him almost immediately. He's wittier than he used to be, takes more vacations and doesn't let anything get in the way of watching the Yankees on Sundays, as he had in the past.

As different as the symptoms, backgrounds, and situations appear to be, all my people suffered from the same bad habit with the same purpose, to eliminate expression. All responded favorably to the same intervention, Attention Training. By simply increasing awareness, symptoms were relieved, since they were no longer needed as a distraction from the environment. With intelligence accurately connected with the environment, threat was not perceived. Without threat, no state of alarm was signaled and symptoms did not occur.

With increased awareness, intelligence increased. My people understood that differences of opinion are points of view. This is the change that makes all the difference for Attention Training. They were no longer forced to hold back expression for fear of negative consequences.

The bad habit was developed by criticism of expression and, at the bottom line, the tendency to take differences personally. With intelligent thought, expression cannot be taken personally. This information frees the individual to express taste as a style in thinking and behavior. The new habit eventually develops into a reflex, which constantly seeks pleasure. I refer to this condition as happiness.

It has taken nearly twenty years to develop the theory of Reflexive Attention Diversion and the technique of Attention Training. From the frustration of treating individuals with little to no progress, to the crude attempts to have my people pamper themselves, to the structure of the Four Points, to the very important concept of taking back small times, it's been a long but worthwhile journey. The change that occurred in my people was a reward for me that few individuals could ever hope for in their lifetimes.

Chapter X

Extending The Senses

"To see the things of the present moment is to see all that is now, all that has been since time began, and all that shall be unto the world's end; for all things are of one kind and one form."
Marcus Aurelius

I want to relate one more technique to you. It isn't one that is necessary to complete Attention Training; it's extra. I have only taught it to about ten of my people since all would eventually reach this stage as the new habit gained strength. Anyway, I thought some of you might want to try it or at least might find it interesting.

Around 1993, although I was well satisfied with the performance of the Four Points, I wondered if I could reduce intervention time even more. I was looking for a way that, when I taught Attention Training to a patient's intelligence, I could teach his body the behavior at the same time. It sounds impossible, but I also once thought that a standardized technique to relieve psychological symptoms was impossible.

I thought about the idea quite a bit. How could I speed up the body's ability to learn a reflex? I knew if a behavior is repeated frequently, especially if the behavior is pleasurable to the body, a reflex could be learned. But how could the body learn the behavior almost instantly. I knew the body could learn the bad habit in a "one shot" learning, as I saw with Bob and so many others. A person whose previous life appeared to be symptom-free could develop horrible anxiety and other symptoms as a result of a trauma, such as a motor vehicle accident.

If the bad habit could be learned by the body in one experience, then why couldn't the process be reversed? This reversal was what I had successfully accomplished with many people as a result of Attention Training. Could the same be done in a "one shot" learning?

The bad habit could be learned instantly if the negative situation triggered intense fear in the individual. The fear was so intense as to impress on the person that negative consequences could happen at any time and be out of her control. This condition led to a fear of the unknown and produced symptoms in any situation that was unpredictable. It seemed logical to me the process could be reversed and used to reduce intervention time.

I learned much from the Four Points. I learned increased awareness was pleasurable to the body. I also learned that my people found nature to be quite pleasing to the senses. This made sense. The bad habit had been learned through pairing expression with criticism from social sources. If awareness could be increased greatly, pleasure would also. If the sensation of pleasure was greatly increased, then the body would be given something to remember and the new habit should be able to be learned quickly.

It was logical that increasing awareness toward any social or people product, situation or event would not produce the desired effect since there would have to be some degree of negative association resulting from criticism. I decided nature would be the most logical situation in which to pair increased awareness with pleasure, since it appeared to be nonthreatening to most individuals. I believed if I could have my people allow nature events to stimulate and to flood their senses, the experience should jump-start the body into forming the new habit very rapidly.

I asked some of my people to attempt the procedure. However, when they tried to extend their senses, they experienced either distraction or some mild anxiety, which was sufficient to disallow them from flooding their senses. It was obvious the old habit was resisting the technique and this situation had to be handled first.

I realized if my people had to reduce the bad habit's resistance, then my hope to teach the mind and body at the same instant would not work using this technique. However, I was attracted to the idea of flooding the senses, so I continued to experiment.

In mid-1994, I decided to work on the technique further, and asked one or two of my people to focus on extending the senses. I had been seeing Jim at the Jersey City office concerning some family problems and he had learned the concept of Reflexive Attention Diversion and Attention Training very quickly and very well.

I explained the procedure to Jim and he readily agreed to try the technique. He had been using the Four Points and taking back small times long enough to have his new habit strong so as to not be affected to any significant degree by resistance from the bad habit. I explained to Jim the importance of using nature and not people or creations produced by people in order to get the effect that we wanted. He told me he had a tree in his backyard that he particularly liked and that he planned to use it to try the technique.

I asked Jim to clear his mind of any thoughts and, when he had, he should allow pleasurable stimulation from nature to flood his senses. He was not to have thoughts concerning what he sensed or try to interpret those thoughts, he was just to experience as much as he could. The idea was to allow so much pleasure into the senses that euphoria would be generated. At the least, a peaceful state of mind would be produced. Jim seemed to understand and appeared quite motivated to try the procedure.

He had mastered every procedure I had taught him in record time. It was as if he had already thought in the style of Attention Training but had not actively employed the procedures. Every technique and concept he learned during our sessions seemed to release the way of thinking that he possessed but which had laid dormant. If anyone would succeed in extending his senses, it would be Jim.

Jim returned for our next session disappointed. It hadn't worked. He told me that he tried the technique about a dozen times with no effect at all. I knew it might require a number of repetitions to produce what I called catching the present, but a dozen times with Jim, who shouldn't experience much resistance, seemed too much.

Jim and I went over his attempts at extending his senses and catching the present a number of times. Finally, it made sense. Jim had practiced the procedure in the morning. He would take a comfortable chair, sit facing the tree, and allow his senses to be flooded, but nothing would happen.

Asking Jim for more details, I found he was in his bedroom in the morning looking at the tree from his window. Jim's property is a corner one so from his bedroom he could see the tree, but also the pavement and the houses across the street, any cars that passed by, and the window itself. It was possible that the view of the street, houses, and cars were sufficient to keep him from extending his senses to the degree necessary to obtain the effect we wanted. I explained my thoughts to Jim, and he agreed to bring his chair outside and in a position where he would only be able to view the tree without interference from the street or any other human or society-related situation or symbol.

Jim came in for his next appointment about ten minutes early. From my office, I could see part of the waiting room. Jim was the only one waiting for me. He was seated to the right of my vision, partially hidden by the wall, which expanded the waiting room from the fifteen-foot hallway that led to my office. I could see his left leg clearly. He moved his leg and the movement somehow seemed more fluid. Not a very scientific observation, but that's how I saw it. Something was different. I realized Jim might have been able to extend his senses.

Jim came into my office. The man literally glowed. Jokingly, he started rubbing the wooden door to the office and behaving as if he had found his truest love. He had the silliest grin on his face, which transformed into a broad smile when he was done with his antics and settled into the chair on the other side of my desk. His first words were, "I did it." I couldn't help but join him in uncontrollable laughter. Once we settled down, Jim explained what had happened.

He told me he tried the procedure on three consecutive days prior to catching the present. He had taken his chair out to the yard and sat looking at the tree, positioning himself with his back to the street. He cleared his mind and allowed the tree to flood his senses. He could smell the fragrance of the grass and growth, see the leaves of the tree move in the breeze, hear the rustle of the leaves and became absorbed by the sensation. He reported he experienced a little nervousness but was left with a pleasant, peace-of-mind feeling. He tried the procedure on the following two days and the nervousness decreased to zero, but he still was left with the peace-of-mind feeling and not the euphoria.

Although Jim was very satisfied with the peace-of-mind feeling, he wanted the euphoria. He was determined and he knew it would happen. On the fourth day, Jim took his chair and sat in front of the tree. He felt particularly relaxed, with a clear mind, and he knew that today would be the day. It wasn't long until Jim felt the beginnings of a thrill deep in his stomach and mid-section. The thrill grew and grew and he caught it. He not only felt wonderful but also experienced a thrill similar to a roller coaster ride. The feeling intensified into euphoria and Jim let it happen. As it subsided into a constant level, Jim told me he still hadn't returned to his pre-procedure status. He said his new habit had taken a huge jump in strength. It had increased in intensity and had stabilized at a higher level. Although it was not at the intensity to create the euphoria, it was at a level that had Jim smiling throughout the day. Jim told me that even previously distasteful situations and events where different. He couldn't take them as seriously as before. His attitude had changed from good to great.

Jim continued to reinforce the procedure. He became able to get the feeling of euphoria whenever he viewed his favorite tree, then to other trees and finally, when he simply thought of the feeling.

Mary was Jim's counterpart in Belmar. She had some confidence problems at work and at home. She, like Jim, understood the theory of Reflexive Attention Diversion and the intervention of Attention Training from the start and made some immediate changes. Once her symptoms were decreased and her new habit was strong, I explained extending the senses to Mary, and she agreed to try it.

At the very next session, Mary came into my office changed. Her expression was more relaxed than I had ever seen. Her movements were fluid and her verbal expression was easy, clear and full of positive emotion. Like Jim, her eyes were alert, alive and glowing.

Although she had done very well with Attention Training and had not experienced any symptoms for quite a while, she wanted to have her mind especially clear before trying to extend her senses. Mary's a runner, usually doing about five to seven miles three or four times a week on the boardwalk in Belmar. As many runners will agree, a run can clear your mind quite well and Mary used her workout for that purpose. After running five miles, Mary walked along the boardwalk. She felt good, refreshed, and clear. She turned away from the traffic on Ocean Avenue and toward the ocean. She could see the waves of the ocean slapping the shore, the gulls cruising the surf for baitfish, the clouds in the sky and the horizon. She could hear the sound of the gulls, the breaking waves, and the breeze on her ears. She could feel the mist from the curls of the waves and the breeze on her skin cooling her from the warmth of the sun. And she could smell the sea air coming off the ocean.

Mary let herself go. She had no holdback. She allowed the sensation to flood her. She didn't interpret or channel the sensation in any way. She simply allowed it to take her wherever it would. Mary felt the euphoria immediately. It began with a thrill deep within her and spread throughout her body. She did nothing but smile and enjoy it. Mary told me that it lasted throughout most of the day regardless of her activity. She, like Jim, felt herself settle into a higher level of the new habit, not as intense as the euphoria, but a pleasant feeling that appeared to be hers to keep.

Mary's increased level of the new habit had her keep things in perspective. She felt happy with herself and those around her and symptoms appeared impossible. She practiced the technique and stabilized her new habit at a level higher than I have seen in most people. Mary ended Attention Training in late 1995. I last saw her in July 2000. She continues to look fresh, relaxed, and glowing with alert, alive eyes.

Although I hadn't discovered how to train the mind and body at the same time, I did get some idea of what truly living in the present and being open to experience the environment is capable of providing; awareness of your surroundings. It is where we should be. To miss moments in the present that you will never get back is the crime of the bad habit. Its purpose is to have you distracted by symptoms. It doesn't matter what the symptoms are, what is important is their function, to disallow your expression to the events taking place around you at all times. The purpose of Attention Training is to increase your awareness so you may witness your life.

Extending the senses and catching the present are extensions of Attention Training. I haven't used the technique with most of my people because it would require additional sessions that they could not afford. I have instructed extending the senses to those of my people who seem to think in the style of Attention Training prior to learning the Four Points and taking back small times and appear to be able to catch the present fairly easily.

Although the technique isn't for everyone, some of my people have tried it and have gained the peace-of-mind feeling. Others have gained the euphoria. What is most important is that each has developed the new habit and has lost her symptoms. Extending the senses may well lead to my idea of teaching the mind and body at the same time. For now, the idea remains a dream.

Chapter XI

The Bon Marché - Revisited

"Principles can only lose their vitality when the first impressions from which they derive have sunk into extinction; and it is for you to keep fanning these continually into fresh flame."
Marcus Aurelius

So what was the significance of the eerie situation with the redheaded woman back in 1968 Was I just being a naïve twenty year old or was the experience as important as I thought it might be? If I had known better, I might have thought I suffered a psychotic break. The fact is I wasn't frightened as much as I was confused.

I had long thought the glazed look in the eyes of my friends and others had something to do with feeling nervous, but my experience went way beyond a glazed look. I actually saw the world as if I were small, a child of maybe five or six. But it was more than just my vision. I knew that it was an illusion. I felt young. I felt immature, dependent, as if I were doing something wrong without knowing what. I felt I would be rejected. I felt like a "bad boy."

Over the years, I knew the illusion had to do with the redheaded woman and how she looked at me. She was seductive, there was no question in my mind about it and I found her attractive. So I knew there was a sexual, or at least intimate aspect to the interaction. I also realized the event happened very quickly. Actually, I was surprised to see the woman at all. I was completely taken off guard. If I had some prior knowledge that such an event might occur, as, for instance, in a situation where men and women socialize, my intelligence would be able to accommodate such an interaction. As it was, there was no time for my intelligence to adjust to the situation at hand. Similar situations, such as surprisingly losing your balance or at the last moment catching an object that was thrown at you without your knowledge, are dominated by reflexive actions since intelligence had not had the opportunity to problem-solve the situation and act.

However, it wasn't until I had developed Reflexive Attention Diversion that I understood what happened at the Bon Marché in 1968. The bad habit isn't a bad habit at all, at least not until criticism is paired with expression to the point that all expression triggers symptoms.

We all grow up with a sensitivity to offending and to be offended. If you can remember your youth, you can remember tending to take items a bit too personally. As children, we all have offended people with tactless expression when we were only intending to state an opinion. I'm sure you all have felt guilt and fear over becoming angry with a parent or even wishing her dead. Can you remember the severe guilt and fear you experienced as a result? A child's thinking is magical. Children believe their thoughts can become reality.

This is because our intelligence has not yet matured. As children, the major characteristics of intelligence have not developed to capacity. We cannot see differences between situations well and, therefore, cannot respond to those differences appropriately.

In my twenty-year-old, Catholic, Italian-American mind, the ability to perceive, understand, and tolerate expression from others was developing, with appropriate responses to follow. However, as a young man with the background I experienced, a seductive encounter took on a very high value. In addition, with the event as a surprise, I was at a loss as to how to behave.

The result of this condition was that I lost intelligence or contact with the environment. It was lost to such a degree and so quickly that the only perception of the world left to me was out of the eyes of the habit at the specific time when it was incorporated into my body as a reflex. Since the habit is usually learned in childhood, I viewed the world as a five or six year old, at the specific time and age when the bad habit was retained by my body as a result of repetition. Most interesting, not only did I view the world as a five-year old child but I experienced the emotions of a five-year old doing something wrong. I felt immature, inadequate, confused, insecure, and nervous and I expected to be rejected. In essence, I actually was a five or six-year old child.

I have met four or five people who have experienced similar events. Most people experience the return to the habit in a less dramatic fashion. For example, you may be with your peers at work, standing and talking, and you may feel stiff, immature, less capable and less worthy than the others, with nothing to say. Let's say you're in a social situation where you may be more yourself and you're talking to someone you find attractive. The value you put on the situation pulls you inside your head a bit and, even though the person is your equal, you feel somehow incompetent and vulnerable, feeling any word you express is sure to be wrong and offensive. You feel and act like a child potentially offending an adult.

The information from the event with the redheaded woman revealed some important information. It indicated that once the habit is learned and incorporated into the body as a reflex, it doesn't really change. If it would, then I would have perceived the environment as an older child or even a young adult. The information that the reflex doesn't change is logical since the body learns a reflex to provide a function efficiently and there would be no reason for it to alter. Nor could it since it is out of conscious control. It is true the reflex could change somewhat as a result of chance behaviors being added to it, but the changes wouldn't be so significant as to cause a difference to the habit as a whole. It would basically remain the same.

The bad habit hasn't changed much since it was incorporated into the body. We're dealing with the same habit that was learned as a child. However, we're not trying to dismantle or replace the bad habit. Actually, Attention Training pays little to no attention to the bad habit. The entire effort of Attention Training is to develop a new habit independent of the bad one. How long you have had the bad habit influencing your expression has no effect on learning the new one except for the resistance encountered toward the Four Points during the first few weeks. Since the new habit is learned independently of the bad one and based on the Pleasure Principle, it may be learned quite quickly.

The most important information I received from the experience with the redheaded woman is there is something more to psychology than I had learned in school. The experience pushed me to try to find techniques that could counter the attention loss that seemed to result in the nervousness I felt at the Bon Marché. The suffering that people like Sandy, Bill, Sarah, Fran and the others experienced further motivated me to try different avenues from the conventional ones many of my people had used with no lasting results. My people taught me what to look for by their symptoms and the experiences they went through with other doctors.

Attention Training has helped many people. It's the only technique I use. The technique is obvious, to the point and effective.

The only criticism I have received concerning Attention Training is that it is too simple. For that, I apologize.

Welcome...

APPENDICES

CONTENTS

...to...

Appendix I

RAD Symptom List

The RAD symptom list is not a scientific test. Instead, the list is provided so you can make a decision as to whether RAD is affecting the quality of your life. It is designed to help you recognize the ways in which decreased attention is converted into behaviors, attitudes and emotions that eliminate your spontaneity and prevent you from living life fully.

While some of you may experience the disruptive symptoms of anxiety and depression, the majority of you do not. However, what is common is for RAD to prevent you from experiencing happiness.

As stated in this book, some of you may be able to build the new habit on your own. Of course, it will take motivation and hard work but if you really want to achieve happiness, the techniques are there for you to use. Others of you will need the help, guidance, and knowledge of a trained professional. Try the procedure on your own, but if you believe that engaging in an Attention Training class would help you learn the new habit sooner, then seek one out and begin learning as quickly as possible. You may find the location of the nearest Attention Training class at my website, www.drmastria.com. Remember, the habit has robbed you of enough time and experiences. Begin living life as fully and as soon as possible.

Symptom List

You may not experience every symptom mentioned below and you may find symptoms you do experience do not occur all the time but in pockets or areas of your life. Symptoms are listed so you may gauge whether the habit is robbing you of pleasure by generating a style of avoidance.

1. I tend to take differences of opinion personally as angry acts or as criticism.
2. I tend to think too much.
3. I worry about the future.
4. I worry about what people think of me.
5. I have trouble making decisions.
6. I hold back what I think for fear of offending those around me.
7. I tend to daze off when reading, driving or watching TV.
8. My vision is sometimes cloudy or foggy.
9. Sometimes I feel distant from what is going on around me.
10. Sometimes my hearing seems hollow.
11. Sometimes I feel numb.
12. I have trouble saying "no" to people.
13. My thinking is usually negative.
14. I feel like running from some situations.
15. I'm usually scattered in my thinking.
16. I believe I have nothing to say to people.
17. I believe what I say will be the wrong thing.
18. I have trouble focusing my attention.
19. I tend to avoid things.
20. I question my decisions.
21. I have trouble concentrating.
22. I have trouble remembering things.
23. I have difficulty falling asleep.
24. I have difficulty staying asleep.
25. I awake during the night with anxiety.
26. I'm tired when I awake in the morning.

27. I feel apprehensive when I awake in the morning.
28. I get irritated over minor things.
29. Sometimes it's like two people talking in my head, one positive and one negative.
30. I don't think people will like me once they get to know me.
31. I don't trust my opinions.
32. My thoughts race sometimes.
33. I tend to procrastinate.
34. I anticipate failure when I try things.
35. If someone likes me, I can't figure out why.
36. Living is so hard I sometimes wish I wasn't here.
37. I don't enjoy life like I believe other people do.
38. I feel edgy.
39. I feel down often.
40. I believe mistakes from the past will affect my future.
41. I sometimes startle awake when I'm drifting off to sleep.
42. I feel stiff and awkward around people.
43. I jump when something unexpected happens.
44. I have anxiety all the time.
45. I depend on others too much.
46. I can't solve problems like others can.
47. I think I'm lazy.
48. I think of myself as stupid.
49. I think of myself as less than other people.
50. I don't think I will ever be happy.

...the...

Appendix II

The Four Points – Short Form

The new habit is built by pairing awareness with pleasure. The Four Points is designed to increase attention in order to produce greater awareness. This increased awareness of the environment produces pleasure. The resulting pleasure is defined as likeable stimulation to the senses. With repetition, the new habit is strengthened and automatically maintains contact with your surroundings, thus reducing the negative thoughts, which generate symptoms. The new habit does not replace the bad one; it competes with it for dominance. Since the new habit is based on pleasure, the body gravitates toward it over the pain caused by the bad one. The idea is simple. If awareness does not reduce as a result of decreased attention, negative thoughts from the bad habit, that trigger negative emotions and other symptoms, cannot be generated.

The Four Points are:

1. *Be Oriented.* Consciously and deliberately be aware of the time, your surroundings and what's going on around you.

2. *Use any or all of the five senses.* Consciously see, hear, smell, touch, and taste. Sense your surroundings. Seeing, feeling and touching are the easiest senses to employ in directing your attention toward the environment.

3. *Be active. Don't allow yourself to drift.* Activity may be any voluntary behavior. Going for a walk, phoning a friend or relative, watching a video, baking a cake, anything. Activity may be the single most important aid to help you stay focused on your surroundings.

4. *If you can't see it, don't think it.* All that you should have on your mind is what's happening in the present. In other words, if you can't see, hear, smell, touch, or taste it, don't think it, it will probably be an out-of-control thought from the bad habit.

The Four Points are to be performed consciously and deliberately throughout the day, moment to moment. As a result of resistance from the bad habit, dramatic results cannot be expected as you begin to use the Four Points, but notice, for the brief time your attention was increased toward the environment, you felt slightly better. It is the conscious connection between increased awareness and pleasure (feeling better) that will build the new habit and rid you of symptoms.

Appendix III

Taking Back Small Times - Short Form

While the Four Points is designed to build the new habit in your conscious thoughts, taking back small times is intended to build the new habit in your orienting thoughts and behaviors, and therefore, in your body. Taking back small times works on the same principle as the Four Points, which is to pair awareness with sensation to produce pleasure. The Four Points is directed toward focusing on more intense objects such as breezes, clouds, color and sound whereas taking back small times is focused on objects and stimulation of a much lower intensity such as sound filtering into a room.

In order to accomplish taking back small times, some portion of your orienting thoughts and behaviors must be converted into conscious ones so that stimulation to the senses may be applied. Maintain your conscious thoughts by focusing on objects while being aware of peripheral information. Don't focus directly on the peripheral information, as you would using the Four Points, but be aware of peripheral information in addition to your conscious focus, not instead of it. For instance, let's say you're focused on your favorite TV program, but aware of the feel of the couch beneath your body, the sound of your wife speaking to your son, the floor beneath your feet, the pressure of your left arm on your thigh and the movement of your right hand rubbing your chin.

While the Four Points works to extend your attention and focus, and therefore your awareness, taking back small times expands your awareness. With sufficient repetition, your finished product will be an extended and expanded awareness that will not allow a decrease in attention and the out-of-control thoughts that distract you from living an enjoyable life and produce more symptoms.

...Present!

Appendix IV

Glossary

The glossary is intended to provide a definition of terms that I normally employ in Attention Training. The purpose of the glossary is to aid in the communication concerning Reflexive Attention Diversion and Attention Training.

Activity - Cognitive (thinking) and/or motor (physical) involvement with one's environment. For Attention Training, activity should be deliberate and intentional, p. 71.

Activity, Active - Voluntary behavior (cognitive and/or motor) which demands active attention and participation on the individual's part. Examples are bicycle riding, swimming, rollerblading, walking, games, etc. Active activity is significantly more demanding of attention than passive activity, p. 79.

Activity, Passive - Voluntary behavior (cognitive and/or motor), which is less demanding of the individual's attention and participation and therefore, more susceptible to the influence of the bad habit in the form of out-of-control thinking, especially avoidant thinking. Examples of passive activity include, reading, driving and TV watching, p. 79.

Anger, Unwarranted - Hostile and aggressive thoughts and/or behavior in response to out-of-control thinking, especially mind reading thoughts, feeling trapped and controlled and the tendency to take differences of opinion from others as criticism, p. 92.

Anger, Warranted - Aggressive thoughts and/or behavior in response to feeling hurt and/or threatened by an event, situation or person. Warranted anger is in response to maliciousness on the part of another, p. 91.

Anxiety - A fear response that has no observable source in the environment. Anxiety requires the individual respond to threat from outside the present in the form of negative anticipation, p. 88.

Attention - The intellectual mechanism that functions to connect and maintain the individual's contact with the environment, p. 32.

Attention Training - The systematic and intentional process of pairing increased attention toward the environment with pleasure for the purpose of producing increased awareness and reduced symptoms, p. 70.

Attitude - A state of mind or style of thinking that may reflect or avoid taste, depending on whether mediated by intelligence or the bad habit, p 39.

Automatic - Action occurring as a result of habit without conscious intent; similar to a reflex; developed from repetition, p. 30.

Autonomic - That part of the nervous system that pertains to involuntary body functions, p. 30.

Avoidant Behavior - Any behavior which functions to reduce anxiety by providing a behavior other than that which reflects the taste of the individual, p. 41.

Avoidant Thinking - The out-of-control thought that occurs in situations of low stimulation and results in decreased awareness occurring as sensory perception recedes from the environment; examples include drifting or zoning out, p. 78.

Bad Habit - Automatic style of thought and behavior occurring as a result of pairing expression of taste with criticism, producing an avoidance of spontaneous expression of taste, resulting in symptoms, p. 35.

Bad Thing - The anticipation that an unknown quality, which is out of the individual's control, will be expressed with negative consequences to follow, p. 45.

Blindsided - The symptoms which occur as a result of being surprised by a rapid decrease of awareness of the environment, p. 118.

Born With - The capacity to behave toward the environment in a certain way, automatic from birth, p. 52.

Catching the Present - The euphoric feeling caused by flooding the senses with stimulation from nature, p. 171.

Changes - Differences in routine that may trigger the habit since possible spontaneous expression may occur and the "bad thing" may be exposed, p. 96.

Changing the Scene - The technique of consciously altering stimulation to the senses in order to reduce mild anxiety, p. 116.

Characteristics of Intelligence - The ability to perceive differences among situations and to respond appropriately to the differences perceived, p. 33.

Clarification - A communication technique designed to gain clearer understanding of another's expression by requesting additional information. Also, a technique to request information to confirm another's understanding of one's own expression, p. 139.

Communication - The clear exchange of ideas through expression between individuals, p. 139.

Compulsion – An insistent urge to perform a repetitive behavior with the purpose to distract the individual from the present so expression cannot occur, p. 41.

Confidence – Automatic knowledge that future events will be handled so that awareness may remain in the current, since concern or worry is unnecessary, p. 160.

Confusion – A state of alarm resulting from uncertainty because of a lack of information. Confusion may spiral to terror should the lack of information pertain to a high valued event, p. 37.

Conscious Thought – Conscious interpretations of perception that lead to purposeful behavior for the benefit of the individual, p. 145.

Constriction – Condition of holdback producing tightness and cautiousness resulting in a lack of spontaneous expression, p 107.

Current – The moment; what is occurring presently; the here and now, p. 33.

Dazing Off – Avoidant thinking. An avoidance of the current through decreased awareness that typically occurs during times of low stimulation or low attraction of the senses by the environment, p. 71.

Decision – An emphatic statement or expression concerning an individual's point of view which reflects the taste of that person, p. 118.

Dependency – The condition where a person who is capable of performing an activity, maneuvers and manipulates another to perform the activity for them, p. 141.

Depression – Condition resulting from chronically doing what you don't want, p. 42.

Depression, Clinical – A condition of boredom and helplessness to gain pleasure as a result of avoidance to behave according to one's taste, p. 90.

Depression, Reactive – Condition of loss resulting from an actual event in reality. Reactive depression tends to lessen with replacement of the loss, p. 89.

Difference of Opinion – Expression of a different point of view from another, reflecting the different taste of the individuals involved, p. 48.

Disorientation – Lack of knowledge of time and place as a result of less information arriving from decreased attention and sensory perception, p. 45.

Drifting – Avoidant thinking resulting from decreased attention during times of low stimulation, p. 71.

Emotions – Biochemical and attitudinal changes occurring as a reaction to thought, p. 39.

Energy – Fuel reserve that allows the individual to function on a behavioral, cognitive, and verbal level to express taste and enjoy stimulation, p. 131.

Expression – An interaction with the environment through movement, speech, and thought that conveys taste, p. 33.

Extending the Senses – A technique intended to promote euphoria and rapid growth of the new habit by allowing the senses to be flooded with intensely increased stimulation from nature, p. 171.

Familiarity – Knowledge of situations or events that allow predictability and the expression of well-learned behaviors, p. 70.

Fatigue – Lack of energy brought on by insufficient rest or expenditure of energy from intense activity; lack of rest from psychological symptoms such as sleep pattern disturbance, tension, anxiety and depression, p. 133.

Fear – Physical state of alarm or arousal resulting from physical threat of bodily or psychological injury, p. 86.

Fight-Flight Response – Born with mechanism that mobilizes the body to fight off or retreat from threat of harm, p. 36.

Focus – Placing attention on aspects in the environment, p. 70.

Four Points – Ways in which one may consciously and intentionally increase attention and, therefore, awareness of the environment, with the purpose of building the new habit. These include conscious orientation, sensory perception, activity, and thoughts arriving only from sensory perception, p. 71.

Free Time – Leisure time when a person can do as she likes, according to her taste, p. 103.

Frustration – Form of anger that occurs when your attempts to accomplish a goal are blocked, P. 91.

Future Thinking – Out-of-control thought that anticipates the future in the negative, triggering anxiety, p. 77.

Grogginess – A fatigued state. That period of time between waking from sleep and full arousal when the habit may have you think out-of-control and generate symptoms, p. 135.

Guilt – The "nasty" or bad feeling that a person should have for conscious malicious acts against another, p. 122.

Habit – An over learned behavior, which, after sufficient repetition, becomes enacted in an automatic or out-of-conscious control manner, when the person is presented with the conditions under which the habit was originally learned, p. 52.

Habit Thinking – Thought process influenced by the habit. The thinking is associative, negative and pertains to personal content, p. 64.

Happiness – A condition where a person habitually places himself in likable situations, p. 128.

Help – A mature request for assistance for one who is temporarily incapable of performing a function for himself, p. 141.

Holdback – Constriction, both mental, through inattention, and physical, through tension, for the purpose of reducing spontaneous expression, p. 43.

Identifying the Enemy – Intelligence's attempt to reduce confusion by finding an event as responsible for discomfort. Results are negative since thought process is influenced by the habit, p. 37.

Illness – Reduction of energy brought on by physical deficit resulting from bacterial, viral or other organic impairment. Generally of a temporary nature, p. 132.

In Control – A condition of increased awareness and information in the present resulting in accurate perception and appropriate behavioral response, p. 115.

In Front of You – Perceiving and responding to the information in the immediate present, p. 72.

Inside Your Head – The condition of decreased awareness when a person experiences negative thoughts associated with events outside the present, p. 127.

Instinct – A behavior that occurs at a certain maturational level without prior learning and aids in the survival of the individual and the species, p. 30.

Intelligence – Born with contact with the environment. Composed of the thinking and physical parts, intelligence comprehends perception of the environment and leads to purposeful behavior for the benefit of the individual, p. 29.

Interest – The development of taste into skills associated with activities that result in pleasure to the individual, p. 31.

Intervention – A systematic attempt to control the effects of the bad habit by initiating an intelligent habit through specific techniques and procedures, p. 77.

Justification – The attempt by habit thinking to find factors outside the present as responsible for the discomfort caused by decreased awareness, p. 38.

Laziness – A mistaken lay term for avoidance, p. 92.

Leaning Out – Temporarily putting aside thoughts and activity to increase awareness and then to return with greater intellectual perspective, p. 116.

Load Up – Consciously increasing awareness prior to entering a situation of pressure, p. 115.

Loose Ends – "Unfinished business;" situations of low value, which have been put off, and which tend to accumulate as an out-of-control attitude, p. 113.

Manipulation – A conscious and/or reflexive attempt to maneuver and control people through deception, p. 141.

Medication – Chemical intervention that may be used to reduce the symptoms of the habit, p. 124.

Memory – The intellectual ability to retrieve information from the past in order to associate it to a current or future situation, p. 81.

Mind Reading – An out-of-control thought which anticipates the thoughts of another in a negative way, p. 78.

Motor Expression – Interaction with the environment involving muscular movement that conveys style, p. 33.

Nervousness – Low intensity fear resulting from an observable event in the present, which maintains some degree of value, p. 87.

New Habit – The intelligent habit; pairing attention with pleasure to form a reflexive tendency to maintain awareness in the environment, p. 70.

Nightmare – Out-of-control thoughts that occur during sleep and may reach fantastic proportions, p. 119.

Obsession – Repetitive thoughts, which occur to decrease focus toward the environment and, in this way, prevent expression of taste, p. 41.

Oriented – Knowledge of time and place as a result of increased awareness of the present, p. 71.

Orienting Thoughts and Behaviors – Well-learned attitudes, thoughts, and behaviors that occur automatically in response to familiar situations. Orienting thoughts and behaviors provide an anchor in time and place so conscious thoughts may leave the present or focus in the current for the benefit of the individual, p. 146.

Out-of-Control Thinking – Negative thoughts that attempt to justify the discomfort of decreased awareness by fabricating a source for the discomfort outside the present, p. 37.

Outrunning the Present – The habit's attempt to remove the person from the present by racing thoughts to the future so expression cannot occur. Outrunning the present is the adult counterpart to hyperactivity in a child, p. 98.

Oversocialization – Condition of constriction for breaking rules that do not exist. Oversocialization is the result of pairing expression with criticism usually during childhood, p. 47.

Past Thinking – An out-of-control thought that has the individual focus on past events in order to justify unhappiness in the present and to reduce the potential of expression. Past thinking generates depression, p. 78.

Pending Doom – An anxious attitude concerning a non-specific future negative event, p. 40.

Physical Part of the Intelligence – The part of the intelligence which maintains contact with the environment and provides perception; the five senses, p. 32.

Planning – An intellectual projection to an actual future event which involves a decision and then a return to the present, p. 81.

Pleasure – Likeable stimulation of the senses, p. 128.

Pleasure Principle – Biologic tendency for an organism to seek pleasure and to avoid pain, p. 70.

Present – The here and now; what is occurring at this moment in time, p. 32.

Pressure – A condition that decreases an individual's energy supply, p. 132.

Procrastination – Avoidance of a decision or the postponing of handling situations, events and items, producing loose ends and contributing to an out-of-control state of mind, p. 113.

RAD – Reflexive Attention Diversion. A reflexive tendency to avoid expression by diverting attention from the environment through distraction by negative thoughts and other symptoms, p. 35.

Recharging Your Battery – Technique of changing the scene in order to restore energy level, p. 124.

Reflex – Automatic response to a signal in the environment without conscious intention, p. 30.

Relapse – A temporary period when the body returns to the bad habit. Relapses occur as a result of decreased energy, p. 129.

Relaxation – The condition of being "yourself" without tension and constriction from the bad habit, p. 94.

Reminiscing – Intelligent thought that focuses on pleasurable past events and then returns to the present, p. 81.

Resistance – The opposition from the bad habit to the intentional behavior of awareness or opposition from the new habit to the bad one, p. 72.

Response – Expression to an event in the environment, p. 45.

Restructuring Relationships – Reorganizing activities and communications with those with whom you're close, in order to maximize the relationship around shared likes and the avoidance of situations of dislike, p. 139.

Second Thinking – Negative thought placed after an impulse to behave as you like, with the result of canceling out an expression, p. 96.

Self – Composed of likes and dislikes producing a style of thinking and behaving that is particular to the individual, p. 33.

Self-Critical – Negative thoughts and attitudes concerning one's character and ability to express; justification not to engage one's taste, p. 43.

Self-Expression – The process of interaction with the environment in a smooth, economical manner, according to one's taste, p. 33.

Selfish – Self-critical thought that expression of taste is a unilateral act, uncaring of the needs and dignity of others, p. 121.

Senses – The physical part of the intelligence involving the perception of the environment by the abilities to see, hear, smell, touch and taste, p. 32.

Skill – The development of automatic behaviors in order to perform an activity economically, p. 31.

Sleep Pattern Disturbance – Interference with restful sleep by a state of alarm that is incompatible with the relaxation necessary for rest; may include insomnia, fitful sleep, light sleep, anxiety while asleep, nightmare and morning fatigue, p. 119.

Slow Down Your Thinking – The conscious focus toward the environment in order to gain perspective. The control of distracting thoughts from the habit to maximize intelligent thinking, p. 100.

Small Times – The periods of low stimulation or activity between two larger or more stimulating events, p. 145.

Socialization – The procedure by which an individual comes to learn the beliefs and attitudes of her group and internalizes the expectations for her behavior, p. 50.

State of Mind – Attitude or style of thinking; a mindset that influences perception, p. 120.

Stimulation – The impingement of environmental events on the senses, p. 117.

Style – Consistent manner of expression of taste that influences movement, thoughts, interests and opinions from which others come to recognize and associate with the individual, p. 34.

Surge – A brief but intense relapse, which occurs during minor lapses of attention, p. 134.

Symptom – Varying degrees of discomfort in the form of thoughts, feelings, and behaviors that result from decreased awareness, p. 67.

Taking Back Small Times – The procedure of converting some orienting thoughts and behaviors to conscious ones so they may be paired with stimulation in order to build the new habit on a reflexive level, p. 153.

Taste – Likes and dislikes common to the individual. The expression of taste develops interests, p. 33.

Tension – Muscular constriction that occurs when the person doesn't believe he is capable of expression with skill and tact, p. 107.

Thinking Part of the Intelligence – That part of the intelligence that possesses the higher abilities such as problem solving, concentration, memory, intent, creativity, humor, planning etc., p. 32.

Thought – The interpretation of perception and motivator of behavior, p. 33.

Trapped and Controlled – The result of depression; the attitude that the individual will continue to do what she doesn't want without the possibility of ever gaining pleasure. Feeling trapped and controlled generates anger, p. 43.

Treatment – Interventions designed to reduce symptoms resulting from various theories of symptom development, p. 67.

Value – Degree of importance placed on an event, situation, person, or thing by the intelligence, p. 133.

Verbal Expression – Conveying taste through learned language, p. 33.

About The Author

Ernest Mastria, Psy.D, is a New Jersey clinical and forensic psychologist with private practices in Jersey City and Belmar. Dr. Mastria learned about people on the multicultural streets of Jersey City where he was raised. His first generation Italian parents taught him the value of hard work, empathy for others and to express his opinion while accepting differences from others.

With a parochial grammar and high school education, Dr. Mastria decided to follow his older sister to Spokane, Washington to attend Eastern Washington University where he earned a Bachelor of Science degree and a Master of Science degree in clinical psychology.

After returning to New Jersey from Washington, Dr. Mastria attended and was awarded a Doctor of Psychology degree from Rutgers University in 1977. He opened private practice in Jersey City and in Belmar.

Dr. Mastria gained a favorable reputation by treating difficult patients referred to him from other doctors and agencies. It was during his years of private practice that he developed his theory of Reflexive Attention Diversion and his method of Attention Training.

Dr. Mastria is currently working on his second book, *The Habit of Childhood*, which converts the Four Points into an innovative program for difficulties experienced by youngsters. His third book, *The Habit of Relationships*, will follow and add to the understanding of human behavior and to the enjoyment of life.